The Inventive Mind

Introduction to:
THE ADHD LEARNING MODEL
How to Succeed with ADHD

By Richard William Wadsworth

2

The Inventive Mind: ADHD LEARNING MODEL by
Richard William Wadsworth

Published by Richard William Wadsworth

© 2017 Richard William Wadsworth

Cover by Niels Christensen.

ISBN-13: 978-1546673194

ISBN-10: 1546673199

Table of Contents

Book Purpose:

1. To help you stop feeling and acting like a person with a debilitating deficit or disorder.

2. To understand that you can achieve difficult academic or technical pursuits.

3. To appreciate the good things about your mind and learn to use them properly.

4. To teach you the skills to be successful in academic environments even with ADHD.

5. To help you know how a learning environment should operate for people with ADHD.

Intended Book Audience

1. People with ADHD who want to understand themselves and what they are capable of.

2. People who want to understand someone else with ADHD.

3. Parents of someone with ADHD who want to help their kids to succeed academically.

4. Educators of people with ADHD who want to know how to teach ADHD students.

How to Use This Book

I highly recommend that you read this entire book. If you struggle to finish reading books, I recommend going to audible and purchasing the audio version, which should soon be available. If you want more than that or need a more engaged experience, I am also planning an online lecture series that goes through the principles in this book and teaches those principles in a video series.

If you are a student who doesn't have time to finish the book right now and you desperately need help not to fail then I have a different recommendation: simply skip to the last chapter and just follow the ADHD Learning Model steps directly as they are presented. I hope that saves the semester for you. Later, when you have more time, I really think you would be benefitted by reading this entire book.

Introduction

Some people struggle with motivation. That was not my problem. I really truly wanted to get good grades. I wanted to be "that smart kid", but despite my best efforts, I could barely pull off getting C's in most of my classes. When I would study, I would try to read the material, but found myself getting nowhere. Keeping my mind focused on the page was near impossible, and when I was able to grit my teeth and clench my fists hard enough to stare at the textbook, nothing I read seemed to stick. I would stare at the page and come away an hour later with absolutely no idea what I was reading. Was I an idiot? What was wrong with me? My friends would just sit down and study, and then go take the test and get an A. Why didn't that work for me?

I have ADHD and I didn't understand then what it took to succeed. With ADHD, determination and raw effort is not enough. Putting in the time is not enough. Having self-confidence is not enough. Studying like other kids just does not work. You may be able to pass tests that way in some scenarios because you may be smart and make good guesses on the test. But relying solely on your intelligence to make good guesses (and not really having properly studied the material) will only get you so far.

To succeed with ADHD, you have to study like a person with ADHD. As someone with this condition, I have discovered that the ideal ADHD Learning Model is totally different and, in some ways, literally backwards from the model used in nearly all academic learning environments. This is a tremendous obstacle to the millions of people with ADHD.

I am going to show you my methods of how to achieve academic success as a person with ADHD. But first, I ought to tell you my story. If you are like me, one of your biggest obstacles is that you have failed so many times that you think success is impossible. Hearing my story may be just what you need to start believing that someone with ADHD can be successful academically. Maybe, if I did, so can you.

12

I had always wanted to be a doctor. Perhaps this is because I was born with Hirschsprung's disease and it was a doctor that saved my life. Doctors were my heroes and my greatest career aspiration. I held on to my dream for a good part of my childhood. With the onset of high school, it began to get embarrassing when people would hear my career goal and reply to me with, "Oh, you must get really good grades if you want to be a doctor." I'm not even sure how many times I heard variations of that statement. Since I obviously didn't have good grades, I would have to admit my low GPA (Grade Point Average). They would tell me, "If you don't get good grades, you can't be a doctor." And they were right.

Though my grades were so bad, I still had ambitions to succeed. I hoped that, maybe, I could compensate for my abysmal grades by succeeding in other areas of my life. I participated in various sports, did plays, and I ran for Senior Class President. The school held the election. When results came in, I found out that I had won!

A few days later, I was taken out of class. A teacher sat me down in a room by myself and explained that there was a minimum 2.5 GPA requirement to be Class President and that my 2.46 GPA was not sufficient for me to maintain the position. When it was publicly announced across the school that I no longer was the Senior Class President, it became difficult not to be embarrassed and ashamed. This kind of humiliation became the theme of so much I did. Eventually, my ambitions of being a doctor were abandoned. I felt that I just did not have what it took. I was insufficient and no matter how hard I worked, I could not accomplish my ambitions.

My projects were always unfinished. I never knew when assignments were due. I would end up guessing on most of my exams because studying was fruitless. I had to take pre-algebra three times. Sometimes I would take so long to complete my tests that an hour after everyone else had finished, my teacher would come to me and say, "You need to turn it in now." Then I would get my test back with a big fat "F" at the top.

Worse, I would accidentally lock my keys in my car nearly every day and my wallet was lost more often than it was in my pocket. Something was wrong with me. After hearing a description of the condition, I knew I had ADHD (Attention Deficit Hyperactivity Disorder). I didn't want to go to get diagnosed because I felt that it would confirm that something was wrong with me. The last thing I wanted was for a doctor to tell me that I couldn't be a doctor. That's like being slapped in the face by your hero.

Not long after high school, I married the woman of my dreams. She was and remains be my best friend and greatest companion. She lovingly puts up with my short attention span and occasional hyper-focus. We went off to college together and took most of the same classes in pursuit of psychology degrees. For the first time, I started having academic success. It was then that I began to develop the first ideas for the ADHD Learning Model, which led to writing this book.

Because my wife and I followed this model, my grades excelled for the first time in my life. I almost had straight A's! As I approached the end of my psychology degree, I had a 3.96 GPA at over 100 credits. Seeing my high GPA gave me confidence in my intelligence; something I had lost a really long time ago. I went down a number of different career path options because being a doctor still didn't seem like it was a possibility for me.

I need to make a quick note here. When I pursued my degree in psychology, I took all of my classes with my wife and we followed a model of study that enabled me to succeed (The ADHD Learning Model). When I started taking pre-med classes, my son was born and my wife had graduated from college. Unlike before, now I was taking all of my classes by myself. I didn't have my wife as a study partner and our effective study methods were no longer utilized. I had to find other people to study with and that was much harder than I thought it would be. Having tutors was a life-saver, but I could only get them about once a week. I did manage to get a few effective study groups together for a couple of my classes, and interestingly enough, those were the classes that I did pretty well in. But I had a really hard time finding solid study partners in the rest of my classes. In these classes I started getting C's again, just like in grade school.

One class that was particularly challenging for me was General Chemistry. I studied SO MUCH for that class. When I went to the testing center for my first exam, I saw it had complex, multiple-step math questions. This was so different the tests I took in my psychology degree. When I tried to do the problems, I would complete the first stage and then go on to the second stage while trying to take the results from the first stage to the second stage of the problem. Somewhere in this process, I would lose track of where I was and would have to start over from the beginning. This repeated over and over again. I grew frantic because I couldn't focus on the problem.

Finally, I asked for a piece of scratch paper and began drawing cartoon illustrations of what was occurring at each step. This took more time, but I started making progress on the questions! After six hours of drawing out and solving problems, I finally finished the test. I turned it in and got a C. I passed!

After, I found out that my classmates had completed the test in only an hour and many had gotten higher grades. Why did I do so poorly while everyone else did so much better and completed it so much faster? After repeating this same experience for three tests in a row, I went to see a doctor about my suspected ADHD. During my visit, I was officially given the diagnosis of ADHD. There was no hiding it anymore.

I'd like to say that I fearlessly blazed the path straight to being a doctor... but the truth is that I slowly and timidly crawled my way towards the field of medicine. I was very intimidated, and rightfully so. I started with looking into nursing programs, then switched to pre-dentistry. From pre-dentistry, I made a jump to Podiatry and took the MCAT. It wasn't until I had applied to, interviewed at, and was accepted to four podiatry schools when I got my MCAT score back in the mail. My undergraduate degree in psychology was mostly a degree that encouraged reading comprehension. Apparently, all of that reading comprehension really paid off for me because I received a twelve on my reading comprehension score. This score combined with my mediocre other scores gave me a competitive MCAT score (a twelve in reading comprehension put me in the 98th percentile for that category). I hadn't even considered the likelihood of having an MCAT score high enough to actually be able to get into medical schools, but now with my high score I had a real chance of becoming a Physician!

I applied to a long list of schools. I was invited to interview at several of them. During my PNWU interview, I was told that they were concerned because I had taken a very minimal number of classes that would prepare me for medical school. I reassured the interviewer that I would work very hard and would be successful. I had no idea how challenging medical school would actually be. If I had known, I would have been much less confident.

However, my answer must have satisfied them because a few days later I got a letter in the mail saying that I was accepted. I couldn't believe it, I was actually on the path to fulfilling my lifelong dream!

When I arrived at school my head got really big. I was doing something I had only dared dream of doing! I felt so smart. I tried to study just like all of the other medical students. I felt like I was already a doctor. I was on cloud nine. My confidence lasted through my studies and through taking my exams, but then it abruptly ended when the first set of exam scores rolled in. My big head shrank about 50 sizes and my confidence deflated to about nothing.

I did AWFUL. I continued to do awful over and over again. I wasn't sure what had happened! Why was I doing so poorly? I was studying just like all of the other medical students! I was putting in the time, but I was drowning in material that I couldn't keep organized or stay focused on.

I sank back into self-doubt. I felt like I was in high school again. I started having panic attacks. "What had I done? I went to medical school? I am way over my head! What was I thinking applying to medical school? I have ADHD, I can't succeed in Medical school!"

On top of this, I now had three kids and all three of them never seemed to sleep. I was in a constant state of exhaustion, getting only about four or five hours of broken sleep and nearly failing all of my classes. I went on the extended study plan and spread my first-year classes out over two years instead of one. My grades recovered enough that I was able to pass all of my classes... barely. I felt like I was still just scraping by.

My brother-in-law, Jacob Ballentine, gives motivational speeches. One day when I was talking to him, he told me a motivational story about stepping up to the plate with 100% confidence to hit a home run every time you swing. I took the message to heart and changed my study strategy.

I started waking up at 4 AM every morning. I altered my study habits. I stepped up to the plate. I planned for success in new ways and with a different mindset. I started to develop and utilize the

ADHD Learning Model. I began coming up with new ways of studying that mimicked certain aspects of what I had done in undergraduate school when I had been successful. I finally found a study group that replicated some of what I had done in undergraduate school. I started coming up with the methods that I will teach in this book. Finally my grades started to improve dramatically. Instead of failing, I started to do much better on my tests. I still wasn't near the top of the class, but I was successful. I did well enough that I wasn't worried about failing anymore.

One difficulty I faced was that I had to spend considerable time altering each lesson into a format that was compatible to the ADHD Learning Model. It took more time, which limited the amount of material that I could study. But that difference was enough for me to succeed. If I had developed my ADHD Learning Model from day one, I would have had so much more success earlier on. But that's okay, because my challenges taught me so much. What I learned has allowed me to write this book. Things that helped me to find out how the ADHD brain really works and learns best to find success.

Since being diagnosed with ADHD, I have dedicated my life

towards trying to understand how to be successful with my

condition, rather than trying to avoid it. After 25 years of being in

educational systems and tens of thousands of hours spent studying, I

have learned what works and what does not.

I have figured out how to study as a person with ADHD and find

success. As my methods developed over time, they have helped me get through undergraduate school, and medical graduate school to become a physician.

This book is for the millions of people out there with ADHD who have struggled academically like I have. I hope that reading this book will equip you with the self-confidence, motivation, and skills necessary to pursue and achieve your dreams.

1. Swimming Bird

Imagine a bird that cannot find much food anywhere except under the surface of the water. Seeing the food under the water is easy, but getting to the food is difficult. Every time the bird tries to go under the water, it begins to drown and has to come up to the surface for air because it cannot swim.

The bird tries catching the food again and again, but can't figure out how to do it properly. The bird used to feel special with its head in the clouds, but after a while, it feels like being in the sky was locking it out of the ocean. Feeling special and working hard isn't putting food into the birds hungry tummy. It eventually gives up on the idea of swimming altogether and relies on the scraps that the dolphins leave behind.

All of this changes one day while the bird flies over the ocean and spots another bird. This other bird dives straight into the water, swims under the surface and comes out with a mouth full of food!

Birds **can** swim! The hungry bird now knows that success is possible! It follows the swimming bird and asks how the bird did it. The swimming bird explains the method: "You can't try to swim like a fish because you are built with wings, not fins!" Swimming is possible, but the swimming bird also says it isn't easy. Learning to swim will require a lot of determination and effort.

Now that the hungry bird knows that swimming is achievable, he has hope. The hungry bird uses the methods he learned from the swimming bird and eventually meets with success!

I am here to tell you that swimming is possible. Perhaps you may never be as good at swimming as a dolphin, but I also know dolphins can't fly as well as birds. We all have our unique aptitudes.

My first goal is that I want you to see that birds can learn to swim. People with ADHD can learn to achieve academic success. Birds have unique gifts. As I said earlier, they don't swim as well as the dolphins, but they have other things that they do well… like flying. Flying with your head in the clouds has its advantages (I will cover that later with a story called "The Inventor And The Replicator"). Dolphins can also fly through the air when they jump, but they don't fly as well as birds. You have a special and unique gift. A free mind. A mind that can soar with imagination. Your mind can do more than just fly. It can also swim.

I once knew a dentist who shared his story about how he had gotten C's in grade school and never thought he could do well academically in college. Then he explained about how he went to college and did very well and was able to become a dentist. I remembered his story throughout my life and hoped that something like this might happen to me as well so I could become a doctor someday. For me, that dentist was my "swimming bird." Someone who struggled like me, but eventually found success. His story gave me hope. I learned nothing of his methods, but I did take courage from his story. Perhaps I can be your swimming bird.

The hard part is that with ADHD, raw effort isn't enough. I've tried that route and it doesn't work. I nearly drowned trying. When we try harder we may find ourselves hitting our head against a wall. I recall instances in middle school sitting by myself at home, gripping my math book in both hands. I stared in rage and defiance at the page, shaking with determination to read and understand what was on the pages. I was so frustrated because I had been sitting in that spot all evening and made absolutely no progress whatsoever. Sometimes the harder I tried to study, the less progress I would make. Many with ADHD feel this way.

Trying and failing over and over can become an attack on our identity. We can either be a failure who is smart, but just doesn't try; or we can be a failure who tries really hard but still fails because they are dumb. Which of those two options would you choose? This is the kind of thing that people with ADHD struggle with. I wrote this book to help "my people." That 5% of the population who has ADHD.

Though effort alone is not enough, I do feel that I have to work a little harder and longer than people without ADHD. I attribute this largely to the fact that learning environments are geared towards people who do not have ADHD. These learning environments are almost the exact opposite of what an ADHD mind needs in order to learn. Can't talk, can't touch, can't move around.

In medical school (arguably the most competitive and rigorous learning environment on earth) I was rarely, if ever, even close to the top of the class on any test. But, I made it through and it was only possible because I had to cater my learning to the methods that I developed in the ADHD Learning Model. I had to change the material into a format that allowed me to learn in the way that a person with ADHD is meant to learn.

When you try over and over and fail again and again, it's tempting to be like that hungry bird and just give up on swimming. Especially if you aren't even sure if success is possible. What you need is some hope and someone to teach you a new approach. You need a swimming bird.

If you have ADHD, it is not an academic death sentence. You have much better chances of meeting with success by using my methods. It won't be easy and you may have to work a little harder than other people, but success is possible.

Tips for Parents and Educators

1. Go see a psychiatrist, psychologist, or primary care provider to see if your child (or you) have ADHD. If they are struggling in school that does not automatically mean they have ADHD. It could be due to other problems, such as a lack of motivation, poor eye sight, dyslexia, low IQ,

language barriers, social factors, home stressors, lack of

sleep, or absence seizures. See a physician to rule out those

other possibilities.

2. If your child is diagnosed with ADHD, give them some role

models of people who have ADHD (swimming birds) to help

them realize that they are not doomed to failure. Help your

child understand that they learn differently, but that does not

mean that they are stupid. Help them feel special and

intelligent. Much of the title of this book, The Inventive

Mind, is designed to protect the self-esteem of those who

learn differently (have ADHD). Use the principles taught in

this book to help them to learn. There are also other resources

out there too. I recommend that you take advice from your

physician about other options.

2. What It Is And What It Is Not

If you have ADHD, or had it as a child, then you may be able to relate with a lot of what I am going to say. A few years ago I was sitting in my medical school building and talking with a fellow medical student. This particular student did not know I had been diagnosed with ADHD. Somehow the subject of ADHD came up in our conversation and that student began to share their opinion about it. They said, "ADHD isn't a real thing, it's just what you call a person who is lazy and lacks self-control. I get bored sometimes, too, and don't want to study, but I just force myself to do it anyways because I'm not lazy."

Is that really what ADHD is? Is it just the character flaws of "laziness" and "lack of self-control"? I do think that some people are lazy and blame it on their ADHD or say that they have ADHD, when they are actually just kind of lazy jerks. But as one who has experienced ADHD, I definitely believe that it is real and is caused by a difference in "brain type." As far as self-control goes, there certainly is an impulsive side to ADHD, which does denote a lack of self-control. It is more of an inclination towards certain behaviors, (such as moving around or talking), than it is a lack of generalized self-control, at least in my experience. However, that does not mean that some people who have ADHD are not lazy and lack self-control, I've met plenty of people who fit that description. Let me use myself as an example and you can decide if I, a person with ADHD, sound like I am lazy or lack self-control.

Throughout medical school I consistently woke up between three and four AM and quickly exercised and then ate salmon and vegetables for breakfast (because it is healthy) after which I studied until I went to class. Then, most days, I was in class from eight AM to five PM and then came home to my wife and kids.

At home, I helped clean the house, spent time with my kids and then helped put my kids to bed. After that was done, I studied until I went to sleep. On a whole I studied for twelve to fourteen hours daily (including class) for six days a week. Does this sound lazy to you? Or like someone lacking self-control?

I do exhibit a degree of lacking self-control when I frequently jump from subject to subject and am easily distracted. Yet, this is not a generalized lack of self-control associated with a character flaw. It is an inclination associated with the symptoms of ADHD.

In certain settings, I carefully avoided telling people that I have ADHD because I was afraid that as soon as they found out, they would suddenly put me into their "label" of a lazy person who lacked self-control. This stigma bothers me quite a bit. So I would like to take a portion of the book to set the record straight.

If you have ADHD and think that you are unable to control your behavior (outside of the symptoms of ADHD), then what you have is a character flaw in addition to your ADHD.

It is my self-control that I have worked very hard to develop. My early morning routine, daily exercise, and healthy diet are just a few things that demonstrate my self-control as a person with ADHD. I think describing me as someone who "lacks self-control" or is "lazy" could not be further from the truth. Yet the moment that someone finds out that I have ADHD, they sometimes impose these labels on me.

Hopefully after reading what I have written, you can separate self-control from ADHD and stop grouping them together in your mind. If you have ADHD, and happen to also lack self-control, hopefully you will not blame it on your ADHD and will take responsibility for your behavior.

I would also like to address another common misconception about people with ADHD: that they lack the capacity to make good decisions because they cannot synchronously use their pre-frontal cortex (the executive function part of the brain).

The lack of synchronous communication to the pre-frontal cortex does seem that it would make it harder for people with ADHD to make decisions based on predictable outcomes (which can result in poor life choices). But, I think that is only when the decision is not pre-meditated and so is not incorporated into their character. By that, I mean that they have not already made up their mind of how they would act in certain circumstances. For example, children do not have very well established algorithms for character-based decision making. I believe my behavior is based on logical desired outcomes. However, I think this is because I have already made my mind up about what kind of person I want to be. What I am trying to say is, the poor behavior often associated with ADHD (from pre-frontal cortex function issues), is often more of a child-aged manifestation than it is an adult issue.

Having ADHD does not define what you do, but it does affect how difficult some things may be for you. I have to redirect my mind about 1,000 times every day. For every hour I spend studying, I probably spend as much time rereading to try and focus on it, or catching my thoughts from wandering yet again. It is a constant struggle to force myself not to interrupt people or make endless comments in class. When I am in a classroom setting, I have joked with my wife that gravity works in reverse with my arm. I actually have to make a concerted effort to keep my arm at my side to refrain from commenting.

Impulse is like an instinct or drive, but impulse does not rob us of our capacity to control ourselves and avoid being *impulsive*. If you are young and have ADHD, try to control your impulses now and it will of great benefit to you as you get older.

I have a strong impulse to engage in a very active way with my material… if my brain thinks it is interesting. If the information is not interesting, my brain is constantly pulled towards items of interest. I shared with you my frustrations in General Chemistry class and how it took me six hours to take most of my tests. Yet in that same class I scored the highest grade on my thermodynamics test. For some reason, focusing on thermodynamics was more interesting to me. When I went to read the chapter, I hyper-focused and every word soaked into my mind. Is this laziness? Is it stupidity? Nope and nope. It's ADHD.

Since our minds work differently, certain things are harder for us to do (and sometimes certain things are easier). **Harder does not mean impossible.** Back then I didn't have my ADHD Learning Model organized yet, plus every learning environment I have ever been in has been geared for people without ADHD. These are obstacles to overcome to obtain success, they are not excuses to submit to failure. I mentioned how I suspected that I had ADHD, long before I sought a diagnosis. Why did I avoid the diagnosis? I avoided the label because having ADHD or needing Ritalin was the butt of people's jokes. People with ADHD are seen as having something wrong with them. I didn't want anything to be wrong with me and so I avoided the diagnosis. I remember talking to many people who had been diagnosed with ADHD. They told me all of their symptoms and I always felt like they could have been describing me. One of the things often described was a physical incapability of reading certain things at certain times. We might be able to read the words, but there would be absolutely no penetration into our minds.

This may sound silly to people without ADHD, but those of us with ADHD sometimes really do have this virtual inability to pay attention to certain things at certain times. I have a cousin who was diagnosed with ADHD who said, "This diagnosis is stupid, all it means is that I can't pay attention to things that I don't want to!" To which my other cousin replied, "Yes... but other people can." It's true. Other people can read things that their brain hasn't arbitrarily decided is not interesting. There are ways around this I will explain later.

When I try to explain what having ADHD is like, the closest I can compare it to is if you have ever stayed up all night and been so tired that you felt like you could no longer use your brain to read or listen to anyone. If you take away the sleepy component, that is a lot what having ADHD is like when you try to read something that is not interesting.

ADHD does not make you incapable of doing things. It just makes it a little harder to do certain things. Earlier I mentioned how I used to lock my keys in my car nearly every day. I eventually found a way around that. I no longer allowed myself to ever close a car door unless I was literally HOLDING the keys in my hand. I am almost obsessively compulsive about this now. I have to be. This is an adaption.

Earlier I also mentioned how I never knew when my assignments were due, I have adapted for this by becoming very organized and putting everything on my calendar and relying on my phone to vibrate whenever I am supposed to do something.

People with ADHD are capable of doing things, but we just have to do them a little bit differently.

Let's review some things:

1. ADHD *is not* laziness

2. ADHD *is not* the character flaw of lacking self-control.

3. ADHD *is not* stupidity.

4. ADHD *does not* make us handicapped or incapable, we can find ways to adapt and find success.

5. ADHD *is not* an excuse to give up on our dreams.

So now we know what ADHD isn't. So what is ADHD then?

WHAT IS ADHD?

ADHD stands for "Attention Deficit Hyperactivity Disorder." What this means is people who are diagnosed with ADHD have been observed to generally have shorter attention spans than other people (this is the Attention Deficit aspect) and also appear to be more active than other people their age (Hyperactive Disorder). I have some issues with this use of the word "disorder" which I will address later. The actual process of being diagnosed with ADHD needs to be done by a health care provider such as a Psychiatrist or Psychologist (or other primary care physicians).

When medical providers make the diagnosis of ADHD they do so based on the below numbered criteria listed in a book called the *Diagnostic and Statistical Manual of Mental Disorders 5th edition* (or DSM-V):

I have struggled with or still struggle with pretty much every one of the below 18 listed items. Most of them have taken adult forms now (I don't climb on my desk during lecture… most of the time anyways).

If you are like me, you may find it a chore just to finish reading these 18 items. The first section of each numbered point in the diagnostic criteria is from DSM-V, this is "**What others see**", or how other people perceive the symptom. The second section that says, "**What I experience**", is what I have written as a person who experiences ADHD, rather than what parents, educators or a physician may observe.

Signs of ADHD followed by experiences of ADHD.

1. What others see: Often fails to give close attention to details or makes careless mistakes in schoolwork, work, or during other activities (e.g. overlooks or misses details, work is inaccurate).

What I experience: I have the most interesting thoughts during class. When the bell rings, I realize that I have no idea what the teacher has been talking about for the last hour. I ask a friend what the homework assignment was on my way out of class.

2. What other see: Often has difficulty sustaining attention in tasks or play activities (e.g., has difficulty remaining focused during lectures, conversations, or lengthy reading). What I experience: I keep getting new ideas of ways to say or do things differently. The ideas excite me so much that I feel compelled try it out.

3. What others see: Often does not seem to listen when spoken to directly (e.g., mind seems elsewhere, even in the absence of any obvious distraction). What I experience: My own mind is fighting with you for my attention, but the things in my own mind are usually SO fascinating, it is almost impossible to ignore them.

Unfortunately, if I don't ignore my own mind, then I am ignoring you. I don't do it on purpose, I promise.

4. What others see: Often does not follow through on instructions and fails to finish school-work, chores, or duties in the work place (e.g., starts tasks but quickly loses focus and is easily sidetracked). What I experience: Often I don't even know that I am not following instructions because I don't know what the instructions are. Who writes instructions anyways?! Did they take classes in "How to write things in the most boring way imaginable"? When I try read instructions I feel like someone is sucking my life force out of my eye sockets. As far as "quickly losing focus on the task", it's usually because I had another idea or became intensely interested in something else. When I don't complete the school work its often because I didn't even know I had school work, or that I had so many other ideas fighting for my attention that I wasn't able to get it done.

5. What others see: Often has difficulty organizing tasks and activities (e.g., difficulty managing sequential tasks; difficulty keeping materials and belongings in order; messy, disorganized work; has poor time management; fails to meet deadlines). What I experience: When I find something interesting or need to get something done, I love to jump in and figure it out as I go. This can be a messy process sometimes. At times I get a bit overwhelmed with the mess I got myself into.

6. What others see: Often avoids or is reluctant to engage in tasks that require sustained mental effort (e.g. schoolwork or homework; for older adolescents and adults, preparing reports, completing forms, reviewing lengthy papers). What I experience: I just don't learn by sitting in front of a book for 8 hours a day. I learn things "hands-on" or by engaging in the material with other people. Why would I sit and endure a task for hours and hours if I know that I will learn nothing from it?

7. What other see: Often loses things necessary for tasks or activities (e.g., school materials, pencils, books, tools, wallets, keys, paperwork, eyeglasses, mobile telephones). **What I experience:** I have no idea how this happens, but it is super frustrating. I must have been thinking about something else very interesting and lost track of it somewhere.

8. What others see: Is often easily distracted by extraneous stimuli (e.g., for older adolescents and adults may include unrelated thoughts). **What I experience:** I will pay attention to the most interesting thing happening around me. Unfortunately that rarely happens to be a teacher talking about something that I am not interested in.

9. What others see: Often forgetful in daily activities (e.g., doing chores, running errands; for older adolescents and adults, returning calls, paying bills, keeping appointments). What I experience: When I fall into my mind and explore the endless roads of discovery, I will suddenly be pulled out of it and look at the clock. Sometimes hours have passed. I totally intended to do what I said I would do. I had no idea so much time had passed. This is often as embarrassing as it is frustrating.

10. What others see: Often fidgets with (or taps) their hands or squirms in their seat. What I experience: I may fidget because I am in an environment in which I am accomplishing nothing because I do not learn in the presented way and its killing me. I probably didn't even realize that I was tapping my fingers.

11. What others see: Often leaves seat in situations when remaining seated is expected (e.g., leaves his or her place in the classroom, in the office or other workplace, or in other situations that require remaining in place). What I experience: I've got to get up and move around because I want to get going and learn things the way that I learn best: actively doing something.

12. What other see: Often runs about or climbs in situations where it is inappropriate (e.g., in adolescents or adults, may be limited to feeling restless). What I experience: Just want to check stuff out sometimes. Plus I'm bored.

13. What other see: Often unable to play or engage in leisure activities quietly. What I experience: Playing is pretty much noisy by definition… at least for me.

14. What others see: Is often "on the go" acting as if "driven by a motor" (e.g., is unable to be or uncomfortable being still for extended time, as in restaurants, meetings; may be experienced by others as being restless or difficult to keep up with). What I experience: I have an insatiable desire to discover things and to work on projects and ideas that are always in my head.

15. What other see: Often talks excessively. What I experience: If I am not talking about it, then nothing that I am learning will stick in my head. Plus I have some really awesome ideas that I want to share with you SUPER bad.

16. What others see: Often blurts out answers before questions have been completed (e.g., completes people's sentences; cannot wait for turn in conversation). What I experience: I get really excited when I realized that I knew the answer or have an idea about what you were saying. Plus, sitting and listening to the second half of a question when you already know the answer is pretty boring and I am trying to stay engaged with the material or conversation, so I am just trying to speed things up a bit so I can keep listening to you.

17. What other see: Often has difficulty awaiting turn (e.g., while waiting in line). What I experience: I have a million things to do, see, experience, and think about and I want to get going on them while everyone is walking like sloths stuck in cold molasses.

18. What others see: Often interrupts or intrudes on others (e.g. butts into conversations, games, or activities. May start using other people's things without asking or receiving permission; for adolescents and adults, may intrude into or take over what others are doing). **What I experience:** I just wanted to share an idea with you.

Tips for People with ADHD, Parents or Educators

1. Your mind is different. Be proud of that. Let your unique mind give you confidence.

2. Your mind is more motivated by discovery than it is with predictable consequences.

3. Have confidence in your mind to try things beyond your current capacity. Naturally we would be drawn to such things, but years of nearly drowning in a cage under the water kills the instinct and shrivels the drive to go beyond.

4. Understand that it might take you a bit longer to learn things than other people. This is because learning something that has already been learned is called replicating. The novelty has already been drained from the task. You will have to force yourself to do it because it will not be rewarding for you... or you can follow my methods explained in the next chapters.

5. Find some way to keep track of your classes and assignments. I have more on that later.

6. Find a good study partner. Oh my goodness, what a difference this can make.

7. Confidence and hard work are often not enough. You need to find other people who have been successful and try to replicate their methods.

8. Turn your learning objectives into projects to try to induce a hyper-focused state. I will teach you how to do this as well. Just keep reading!

9. If you are a parent or educator of a person with an inventive mind, try to be patient when your kids hyper-focus. Interrupting it can be futile (you may hold their wings down, but their mind will still be on the thing that they are trying to work on). Trying to stop it may just prolong it. Sometimes you just have to let it run its course so it can end as quickly as possible. Appreciate that this is the way they learn best (even if it isn't what you want them to learn right then).

10. Help protect your child's self-esteem! I cannot make this point enough. Realize that everyone is likely tearing down their self-confidence. You can help by believing in your child's intelligence and expressing this belief to them.

11. Help your child to think about their futures. This will demonstrate that you believe that they are capable of achieving success. Having someone else believe in you can make all of the difference. Thinking about their future can also help them to be motivated to do well in school.

12. Sit down with your child after class and do their homework with them one-on-one. If you can't do that, then help them find a tutor or talk to the teacher about getting other resources. If you child doesn't have one-on-one time to study with people, they are likely going to do much worse in school.

13. Recognize that even though your child may not appear to be paying attention to anything that you are saying, they will still somehow learn. I am not sure how this occurs, but it does. Just be understanding that they are going through their own process with the information and taking it at their speed. This can be painful for others to observe. Be patient with their process.

3. The Inventor and the Replicator

My hope for you in reading this chapter is that you will quit hating and being angry at your ADHD brain, and learn to appreciate instead. It's time to start loving the piece of machinery that you were born with. It is true that it is different than most other peoples brains. That makes it unique and wonderful. Many people with ADHD feel like they have something wrong with them because they have a "disorder." I am here to tell you that you can stop that line of thinking right now. Your brain is actually a gift and that makes you gifted.

Earlier I mentioned that I did not like the word "disorder" in ADHD (Attention Deficit Hyperactivity "Disorder"). To me "disorder" denotes that something is out of order, like there was some kind of mistake made when their brain was created or evolved. I think ADHD would be more accurate if it was called ADaH "Attention

Deficit and Hyperactivity." I believe that the ADHD brain has perpetuated in the gene pool for a reason.

It is estimated that about five percent of the general population has the ADHD diagnosis. Once given the diagnosis, they are labeled as "deficient" and having a "disorder."

Parents of kids who have been diagnosed with ADHD are often devastated. Kids can feel like someone just crushed all of their hopes and dreams. Their self-esteem often takes big hits and they sometimes develop Oppositional Defiant Disorder (ODD). I theorize that ODD, a frequent disorder, is likely a result from the fact that kids with ADHD are constantly having people tell them what to do. But they feel incapable of doing what they are asked to do and so they get fed up with it. Defiance is the result.

I believe that ADHD is not a "disorder" at all. My extreme difficulty to focus on monotonous behaviors with predictable results actually has great value. It drives my mind to think outside of the box and to discover new things. However, even when we have something valuable, if everyone tells us throughout our lives that what we have is not valuable and is a mental disorder, we lose confidence to go where our hunger for discovery takes us. Many of us do not offer what we have to the world because we are so often told that what we have to offer is a "disorder."

I theorize that ADHD has a purpose, or at the very least, it fulfills a vital function to society and mankind as a whole. The brain that lacks the ability to sustain attention on things that are monotonous and predictable has the capacity to advance society and technology in ways that are much more difficult for other brains. I think that the way that this advancement can take place is best illustrated in the form of a short story, which I have called:

"The Inventor and the Replicator"

Adah lived in a small village next to a large lake. His clan survived by catching fish with their hands, as they had done for many generations. Most of the group were pretty good at it. Their survival depended upon their ability to catch fish.

Every day the fish-catchers would go out and chase fish all day in the deep water. It was a very monotonous task, but by replicating the same activity over and over, they would become master fish-catchers who kept the clan fed and alive.

Then there was Adah. When Adah's father first let Adah catch fish with his hands, Adah was excited and enjoyed fish catching… but after a time his interest faded. Soon the monotony of fish catching became drudgery. The idea of catching fish for his entire life felt like a death sentence. He would daydream about all kinds of things.

When the other fish catchers saw Adah staring into space, they would become angry and impatient at his "laziness." He would space out when fish would swim right in front of him and his father became embarrassed at his son's obvious "stupidity."

Adah knew that there must be a faster and more efficient way of catching fish... Something less boring. Adah would watch the bugs dance on the water as he daydreamed. He noticed that the fish would congregate out in the middle of the lake where there were the most bugs. This was also the most difficult place to catch the fish because the water was the deepest. One day Adah had an idea. Rather than catching fish, he tried to catch bugs. The other fish-catchers yelled at him. Adah was extremely focused on catching the insects. "We are not bug-catchers, we are fish-catchers!" said his father in frustration. "Get to work or you will get no fish for dinner tonight!" Adah spent the rest of the day in the lake. When he wouldn't catch any fish, his father would say, "Watch me... this is how you catch a fish," while Adah pretended to be interested.

Adah couldn't sleep that night, and as soon as the sun came out he spent all morning gathering different kinds of insects and throwing them in the shallow water where it was easy to grab the fish. The fish would come over to the shallow waters where he could easily snatch them and toss them to the shore.

Before too long he had heaped up a pile of fish. When the other fish catchers arrived, their jaws dropped. "Adah! How did you catch so many fish?!" Adah beamed with pride. He showed them his pile of insects. He showed them how to lure fish to the shallow water with the bugs. Soon all of the fish-catchers began gathering insects in the morning.

Adah's boredom with monotony led to his thinking outside of the box rather than just replicating behavior with predictable and observable outcomes. If his brain had been like everyone else, he would not have had the motivation for discovery. He would have had the motivation to catch fish in a way that would certainly yield predicted outcomes that were understood by synchronous communication between the pre-frontal cortex and the posterior cingulate gyrus (the way a non-ADHD brain usually works). But the ADHD brain does not have synchronous communication between the prefrontal cortex and the posterior cingulat gyrus and so monotonous activity (the kind of activity that yields predictable results again and again and again) cannot be processed in the same way. This pushes the ADHD brain to be inventive and discover new ways to do things. New ways to do things in a manner that has unpredictable results that are not able to be processed in the prefrontal cortex yet.

Now back to our story.

People in the clan had more time to build larger buildings and plant seeds. After a while, Adah, our inventor became bored again with gathering insects all morning and doing the same thing over and over. Everyone else in the group became much better than him at gathering insects and catching fish in shallow water so he started to daydream again. He watched the other fish-catchers snatching fish in the shallow parts of the river. People once again became angry at how few fish he caught compared to them. As he watched them, he imagined their arms getting longer and shooting into the water. He had another idea. He ran into the trees and got a stick. Once again, everyone yelled at him about wasting time. He sharpened one end and carved some barbs in it. He eventually found he could stab the fish with his sharp stick. Yet again, he was catching more fish than the insect-luring fish grabbers. He would lure the fish to the shallow end where he would spear it and fling it onto the shore, only to stab another fish minutes later. People were amazed at this new technique.

Soon everyone was replicating his barbed sticks, and soon everyone was better at replicating the technique than he was. When he got bored of that, he later developed a trap that would catch the fish. Sitting and replicating the same activity over and over again was just too monotonous and uninteresting for Adah.

I should mention that the vast majority of his ideas were not successful and lots of his ideas were never finished because he would move onto a new and more exciting idea… He does have ADHD after all.

Most people in Adah's group were "replicators." They became fantastic fish catchers, insect gatherers, stick-stabbers, fish trappers, and whatever else. They are replicators because they replicate the same activity over and over to yield the same predictable result. This behavior is essential to the survival of the group. Remember how I pointed out that most of Adahs ideas were failures? If everyone sat around trying to think of short cuts and trying to do things "out of the box", we would have few fish "in the box." If you want someone to operate a fish trap, then replicators are the ones you want to hire because they will use it again and again and become masters of its use. They become experts and masters because they are able to devote their entire lifetimes to the same craft. They are masters of thinking inside of the box and mastering a trade. You want most of society to be replicators.

Then much less frequently, you have an inventive mind (a term that encompasses a mind that is creative, constantly seeking change, thinking outside of the box, not content with monotony, and seeking discovery more than a predictable consequence). I don't want people with ADHD to think that they have to be inventing things all the time. It just means that their brains are not well-suited for monotony, and so they are driven towards other paths or doing things in different ways.

ADHD brains (or "inventive" brains) are not as essential to the survival of the group in the short term, but they are essential to its advancement. Inventive minds find doing the same monotonous thing for hours on end to be incredibly boring. So much so, that it is almost unbearable. They have to think of a new way to do things.

Their brain is bored inside the box so it must go outside of the box to find sufficient stimulation. Inventive minds are different. Repetition may drain them, but give them a new idea and you will find that they become obsessive in their hyper-focus and discovery. If you have ADHD, be proud of it! Be thankful for it! You have an inventive mind! You are driven by discovery.

Unfortunately, things are a bit harder for inventive minds than they used to be. In today's society, we have amassed so much knowledge and invented so many things with such an ease of sharing the inventions that most of the low hanging fruit (inventions) has already been gathered (the easy inventions are already invented).

In order to be productive, inventive minds have to go through a very rigorous educational system in order to learn enough information to permit them to produce useful inventions and come up with things that are helpful in our complex society. But there is a problem, learning from other people usually means hours of drudging monotony. Inventive minds finds monotonous activity unbearably boring. Sadly, most of our education system is designed for replicators (minds that thrive with monotony and repeated behaviors). People with this type of mind are completely fine with hour after hour of repetitious activity. The repetitive education system sets up the inventive mind for failure.

Worst of all, kids with inventive minds are constantly judged in school by their ability to sit and replicate like the replicators. That is like judging the bird at how well it can swim. "That bird can't swim as good as the fish, it must have a *disorder*." That is nonsense. As I have said before, ADHD is not a disorder. It fulfills a very important purpose. Replicative minds do things the same way again and again, while inventive minds try to find as many ways possible to do things in new and different ways. Their constant shifting interest and powerful drive to test boundaries and limits with their hands is what promotes change and improvement. There is nothing wrong with you because of your ADHD.

Truth be told everyone's mind is part replicative and part inventive. Most people have minds that are more replicative than inventive. People with minds that are predominantly inventive may not do a very good job at replicating. Their minds just aren't made for it. The current school system is going to be rough for them. Help them to understand that this is definitely does not mean they are stupid.

There is a solution. Education does not have to be a death sentence for kids with inventive minds. Some birds can actually swim very well, but they do it differently than a fish. Because education is designed for replicators, it takes longer and requires more effort for an inventive mind to adapt and survive under the sea in a replicators arena, swimming among the coral reefs for hours on end. Education can be designed in such a way that a person with an inventive mind can make it through to succeed without drowning.

If you have ADHD (and that is the reason only that you are struggling in school), I want something to be abundantly clear. I may repeat this several times throughout the book to ensure that it sinks in. Just because you aren't as proficient as others at doing insanely boring things for hours upon hours and for years upon years, does not mean that you are stupid or that you are incapable of being successful in life.

Your unique brain has the perfect "mental set-up" for discovery. Just as a bird has the perfect "physical set-up" for flight. The fact that you are bored with monotony is the very thing that makes you perfect for finding new things and new ways of doing things. Don't be angry with yourself if you don't score at the top of the class. The main thing that your grades represent is your skill at "replication." It has basically no representation of your abilities to be creative, discover, and invent. Do your absolute best to learn as much as you can and get the best grade you are capable of, but do not label yourself as an idiot if your swimming score is not as high as the dolphins. Your grade isn't on your performance as a flyer. A bird that can swim has the ability to daydream and discover, but then also go down into the water and accomplish what needs done. Your academic learning is vital towards your success. Don't quit or give up just because you don't get top scores or because its painfully boring. Boring as it may be, academic education may be essential to your success.

The fact of the matter is my theory about the usefulness of the inventive brain is pretty hard, if not impossible, to prove. But although it may or may not be proved as correct, it is useful. It is useful because it helps people with ADHD to have confidence and pride in their own minds. Lacking confidence in your mind is extremely damaging to your mental performance. I have gone through so much my life doubting the capacity of my mind. When you learn to love your mind and trust it and have confidence in its abilities and unique qualities, then you are more likely to try and accomplish great things. When I say that, I think about my dad and how inventive minds are still a needed asset in today's world. I would like to tell you my dad's story.

My Dad's Story:

An Inventive Mind at Work in a Modern World

My father has been an inspiration to me throughout my life and I owe much of my retained self-esteem to his example. My dad also has ADHD, though, much like me, he avoided the diagnosis. My dad never excelled academically. Regardless, he became successful. All through grade school he could barely get C's. Sitting and listening to lectures all day was painfully boring because the environment did not allow him to learn in the way that an inventive mind learns best. The only class he ever excelled in was woodshop where he had the opportunity to use his hands and his creativity to make all kinds of things. He did manage to graduate from high school.

My dad had confidence in himself, and due to his constant shifting interest and drive for discovery, he was always picking up new skills. He learned hydraulics, welding, woodworking, fiberglass, electrical work, and all kinds of other handy abilities. He also learned how to be a very successful commercial fisherman.

My dad noticed that often times the fish would congregate in shallow waters where the boats could not go. To overcome this, my dad designed a very light fiberglass boat that had a very flat bottom. This allowed him to bring his boat right up in the shallowest of waters.

Having a shallow-draft boat allowed him to catch fish that no other boats could. My dad made a lot of money catching fish with his shallow draft boat.

Later he fished for herring and noticed that the fastest boats that got to where the biggest schools of herring were, made all of the money. He realized that he had to make a boat that was much faster than all of the other boats so he could get to the fish first. To make a boat that fast he would have to completely rethink the way the boat was designed. He designed a jet-propelled fishing boat with an oxygen intake through the crows nest that could bend down, complete with a skiff ramp so he could put his skiff on board, allowing him to get to top speeds without the extra drag.

He thought outside of the box. His confidence in his own mind and his drive for discovery led the way for him to try new things in new

ways. He had the skills to do all that he did from his constantly shifting interests and ambition to learn with his hands. He designed the fastest commercial fishing boat in the world and was on the cover of *Alaska Fisherman's Journal*, and was awarded as high-liner of the year in 1999.

As the years passed he noticed that the price of salmon was

dropping. Canned salmon wasn't valued as highly as it used to be and getting fresh salmon to market was not an easy process. Most salmon sent to market was frozen at sea, then shipped to a third-world country, where it was thawed and a bunch of workers would

RAY WADSWORTH: IF YOU NEED IT, BUILD IT

M/V Wild Salmon
Sequim, Wash.

pick out the pin bones by hand, then the fish was refrozen and shipped back to the United States. All of that freezing and thawing was making the fish taste... well... fishy. He realized that he needed to rethink the entire fish processing industry. His mind got to work and realized that if he could invent a machine that could remove the pin-bones from salmon, then the fish could be processed without being shipped to third-world countries. Removing these extra steps would prevent the fish from being frozen and thawed multiple times and help it retain its freshness. He proposed his idea to the state of Alaska Science and Technology Foundation and was awarded a two million dollar grant to develop the technology. With a group of engineers, he designed the technology and the machine worked well.

He then designed something called "living fish pens" where fishermen would store the live fish they caught in a giant net next to the processing vessel. They would remain there until the very instant that they were ready to be processed. My dad produced a salmon product that was boneless and the freshest in the world. It had only been frozen one time moments after it was processed. His fish was the most delicious and wonderful fish many had ever tasted because it was so fresh and had no pin bones.

The "big shots" in the fishing industry saw my dad as a threat and his ideas were resisted. People tried to find ways to sue him and destroy his company. This kind of resistance to new ideas is common in all industries throughout all ages. I bet the candle-making industry resisted the marketing of the light bulb in similar ways. Change is often met with opposition.

The world wasn't ready for my dad's ideas quite yet and ultimately, the large businesses in the processing industry are still making plenty of money by shipping their fish to third world countries. Or in terms of my story earlier, the fish grabbers feel good about the amount of fish they are catching using their old methods.

My dad didn't achieve everything he set out to do, but he did tread the way for others to follow. He invented new technology, designed and built many boats, and is a top notch fisherman. He accomplished all of those things on top of being a wonderful husband and father. One thing about my dad is that he can do just about anything. He has been driven to discover so many things with a hands-on approach, that he has learned an insane number of skills.

My dad was always thinking outside of the box. Thinking creatively and driven by discovery. Learning in a classroom environment was not the way he learned best. In the classroom he got C's, but that does not mean that he is not intelligent, gifted or capable. Not all "inventive minds" have to invent things. The ADHD mind is well suited for invention because it thinks of exceptions, resists doing things the same way, and struggles with monotony. An "inventive mind" suggests creativity, ingenuity, and unique approaches to things.

Tips for Parents and Educators:

1. Think long term. In grade school, I earned mostly C's with several D's and the occasional B. Yet, I had an A average in undergraduate school and went to medical school. For some people with ADHD, the ability to use their prefrontal cortex may develop later in life. Be patient and help them to be patient. Just because they can't do something now, doesn't mean that they will never be able to.

2. Your main focus should be to help a person with ADHD to make it through school and life with a good self-esteem and encourage them to discover and explore their educational and career interests. My interests have changed many times. Remember that people with ADHD learn best by experiencing. Remember the story of my dad picking up all of those various skills. I myself have had 14 different jobs and pursued about 9 different career paths before having the courage to become a doctor. This twisty, side-tracked path I took has helped me immensely.

3. Remember to make things into projects. Help people with ADHD to see the light at the end of the tunnel with the projects. Some days you won't make much progress, but any progress is still progress.

4. The Inventive Mind is Discovery Motivated

In order to create a learning model for an inventive mind you need to understand how an inventive mind works. Inventive minds are driven by creativity. Creativity, denotes creation, the drive to make things. Inventive minds are driven by reward-based and project-oriented accomplishments. They are driven by discovery.

The most important question that needs to be answered before any learning can occur is "why." Inventive minds quickly push aside things that do not matter to them because they are always searching for the heart of the problem so that they can get to work and solve it. An inventive mind will start by identifying a problem. Then their brain gets satisfaction through accomplishing something, such as solving the problem or finishing a project. Their discovery-motivation manifests as novelty-seeking and boundary-testing. Ever wonder why ADHD kids often break rules? Part of it is that they aren't always as gifted at picking up on the consequences of their misbehavior (which is kind of a pre-frontal cortex thing rather than an ADHD thing), but it is also because they want to discover what will happen.

It is only by searching through new things and testing boundaries that new discoveries can be made. This is what often gets inventive minds into trouble, but their mistakes can be their friends. That is how invention occurs, through numerous repeated failures. An inventive mind will learn through this process of trial and error and that is how information sticks in their minds.

I have noticed I often need more exposure to learning material for the information to stick. I think this is because I need additional exposure after I have met with failure since it was that failure that motivated me to learn. Failure makes the mind sticky.

Let's contrast an inventive mind to a replicative mind once again. I repeat some of these ideas in hopes that the information will sink into the reader (likely someone with ADHD). Replicative minds are aimed towards achieving a predicted consequence. Replicative minds watch or learn how something is done and then they do it.

They do it again and again and again until they master it and then they keep doing it… this is complete torture for a person with an inventive mind, but this is how 95% of the population learns because 95% of the population has a replicative mind geared towards mastery, and that is good. Monotony, rather than novelty, is the object of the replicative mind. You want a person with a replicative mind to do your heart surgery, or really to do anything that requires a high level of skill, because they will have done a certain task so many times have mastered it.

This does *not* mean that a person with an inventive mind cannot be a master, it just means that their brain will not be as motivated to become a master so it may be harder for them to achieve mastery. It also does not mean that a replicative mind cannot be inventive, it just means that it might not be as motivated to do so. You may want a person with a replicative mind to perform your heart surgery, but what if you have an unusual case that would require discovering a new way of doing things? It will take a mind with a highly inventive component to think of new ways to perform the heart surgery to advance the field. Ideally you would have replicators performing the surgery most of the time and then inventors thinking of new ways to do things and make things better, once and a while.

Because a replicative mind engages in monotony to achieve replication and mastery for optimal outcomes, they tend to struggle with and therefore resist change. This was very evident in my classes whenever something about the course would be altered. Almost regardless of whether the change was a good or bad thing, it was met with hostility and great frustration. I liked the idea of the change, almost regardless of whether it was good or bad. Change stirred the pot for my mind and made things more interesting. It increased the likelihood of me discovering something new. You see, because the inventive mind seeks novelty to achieve discovery and invention, it needs and therefore, initiates change.

Why "Inventive" and "Replicative"

Some people may wonder why I use the word "inventive" to describe an ADHD mind and why I use "replicative" to describe a non-ADHD mind. I know I have covered this some before, but it deserves some additional explanation.

I have several reasons for using the word "inventive" to illustrate the mind of a person described with ADHD. This does not mean that they are always inventing gadgets or something like that, but it does denote the motivation of discovery.

When faced with a task, there are two basic approaches. One approach is to repeat a way that has been proven to be effective in the past. This is replicative and it is consequence-driven and rooted in the pre-frontal cortex. Another approach is to try to create or find a new way to solve the problem, this is inventive and it is driven by the emotional reward associated with novelty and discovery. It really does make more sense to not "reinvent the wheel" and do things in a way that has been proven to work (which is why most people operate that way... except people with ADHD). Going back to the story of the inventor and the replicator, the old way of grabbing the fish had been the method that kept the village alive for generations. You really need to have most of your population be replicators or else people are going to starve.

Inventive thinking is thinking that occurs "outside of the box." Inventive thinking works in processes that result from trial and error and getting hands-on experience. You cannot experiment by sitting and reading about things. Daydreaming is as close as you can get to inventing without touching something. Perhaps that is why inventive minds daydream so much when they aren't allowed to talk or touch things in classroom environments.

The inventive mind just wants to find out what will happen if it does "such-and-such thing." This is a great way to get into trouble... it is also a great way to discover things. It is how a person with an inventive mind works.

Perhaps most importantly, I use the word "inventive" because it helps with self-esteem. Invention denotes intelligence. People with ADHD often feel labeled as "not intelligent" because they don't tend to perform as well on standardized tests (aka, they don't replicate as well). If I could do one thing for people with ADHD, it would be to help them gain some confidence in themselves after going through over twelve years of schooling and constantly getting bad scores and feeling the "label" of it all. Yes, it is true, people with ADHD do not learn well in a lecture-based environment, but that doesn't make them stupid. I have felt stupid for much of my life and I don't want that to happen to others just because their mind is inventive and not replicative.

I use the word "replicative" because a person with this kind of mind is consequence driven and so they are striving to replicate an activity in order to attain a predictable result. Replicators become masters of a skill. If they are able to replicate their skills with great proficiency then they get the predicted result. Their motive is to repeat the same activity over and over because they want the same result over and over. An inventive mind finds much less satisfaction from this because there is no novelty or discovery in repeating a behavior. Once an inventive mind knows what is going to happen, any process can become painfully boring.

Alright, I think I have beaten that horse to death. Now let's talk about what to do about it. What the inventive mind needs is free range. You need to put a lot of material in front of them and then let them shift from one subject to the next. Changing subjects rapidly is actually a really good idea. If you are teaching a child with ADHD, you might spend 5 minutes doing ABC's then 5 minutes doing 123's, then draw some pictures, then sing some songs, then go back to the ABC's again. This recreates the novelty-type experience for the ADHD brain. Let them have some say in the direction of their attention. For a child you might offer three options of subjects to learn. If you are an adult, you might give yourself three subjects to study from and allow yourself to switch between them as your interest changes. As a medical student, I found more success when I switched topics every 20 minutes. If I didn't, my brain would get stale and dry.

You also need to be very careful not to partially engage in your material. I made the tragic mistake of watching hundreds of educational videos as part of my board prep. I thought I was learning, but because I was not engaging my brain in the material properly, I was probably daydreaming more than studying. The data didn't sink in very well, and I did awful on my first board exam. For my second board exam, I found a teaching resource that has a 10 minute video of someone drawing things on a white board, followed by flash cards and then practice questions. The 10 minute video is just the right length for me to still initiate the "discovery" component. Then flashcards and practice questions mix things up and also help my brain continually feel that it is discovering new things in new ways. I am able to study much longer and with much better retention, and without as much daydreaming.

When you are in school, it is a very good idea to read the textbook for a few minutes, then write a few things down and then talk about the things you wrote down with a study partner. This switching of tasks helps you to stay in "discovery mode" as you engage in the material in different ways. If you find your brain starting to get bored, open a different textbook from a different class and study from there.

Mix the pot once and a while. Sometimes when you study, use flash cards. Or make practice questions out of the material. Sometimes make pictures that help you remember things. Always try to reward that discovery-based drive within you through novelty. Don't be afraid to be creative and come up with new ways to do things, too.

The Engagement Criteria and The Algorithm of an Inventive Mind

The Inventive ADHD is not a condition of lowered intelligence. Rather, ADHD changes the algorithm for what directs intelligence compared to that of a person with a replicative (non-ADHD) mind. With inventive minds, the most interesting thing will win their attention. Frequently the most interesting things available are the thoughts inside of their head. This results in daydreaming.

If the person with ADHD is able to engage with the subject (verbally or physically), it can sometimes become sufficiently interesting to maintain appropriate attention. The person with ADHD is then often able to maintain interest on the engaged activity because the act of engaging in that activity is more interesting than the thoughts inside of their head. Engagement has a higher likelihood of meeting certain criteria necessary for attention-directed intelligence.

What is it about an activity that allows it to become engaging? Novelty, discovery, potential or capacity for contribution, creation, creativity, and invention. If the subject does not have a high enough level of any of these criteria then it is likely to be less interesting than the thoughts inside of the head of someone with ADHD and so engaged direction of intelligence will be lost.

The key in teaching a person with ADHD, is to learn how to engage

Engagement Criteria for an Inventive Mind
Discovery (unknown consequences)
Novelty (change and newness)
Contribution (interactive-based, something to give or add)
Creation (project-based, completion reward)
Invention (problem-based, combination of all of the above)

them properly to direct their intelligence towards the desired subject. This can be accomplished by following the principles taught in this book.

Another method that is commonly used is medication. Stimulant medications, when properly prescribed by a licensed physician, can significantly lower the necessary threshold for meeting the criteria (discovery, contribution capacity, invention, etc.) necessary to maintain engagement and direction of intelligence. When stimulant medications are appropriately prescribed by a licensed physician, it lowers the criteria threshold of the inventive mind so that it does not take very much for them to find the adequate stimulation necessary for the direction of their intelligence.

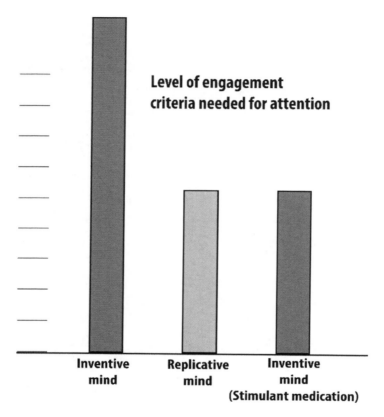

Level of engagement criteria needed for attention

Inventive mind

Replicative mind

Inventive mind (Stimulant medication)

Note about graph: Earlier I mentioned that no person is 100% replicative or 100% inventive. So even people with a much more dominant replicative function do need some degree of engagement criteria, though the requirement would be lower than that of a person with a predominantly inventive mind.

So for people with more dominant inventive function, only activities that meet higher levels of the criteria for engagement will provide adequate stimulation for directed intelligence.

Thus, properly used and prescribed medication use can allow a person with a predominantly inventive mind to be adequately engaged with tasks that have lower levels of novelty, discovery, capacity for contribution, creation, creativity, and invention. The medication does not destroy the capacity for activities that exhibit these characteristics, but it does lower their drive and ambition to obtain them. Thus, these kinds of activities are not as likely to be sought after.

Let me provide an example:

I was finding it almost impossible for me to study for my upcoming board exam because my mind was full of thoughts regarding my book (a subject that, for me, has very high levels of novelty, discovery, contribution capacity, creation, creativity, and invention). Whenever I would stop studying, my mind would immediately go to my book and make massive strides towards its completion. My mind became so irresistibly drawn to the high levels of the engagement criteria found in my book that studying for my board exam became almost impossible.

When I am in this kind of circumstance (which is a frequent occurrence for me), I could likely find adequate engagement if I were to have a study partner. Thus meeting the requirements of the ADHD Learning Model. However, no study partners are available to me. I made videos, which helped a lot, but the videos, alone, were not sufficient to study at the level I needed in order to perform well on the board exam. What I really needed was to have a two-way conversation about the material to keep my mind engaged. Without that interaction-based aspect of the ADHD Learning Model, I sometimes found it too difficult to study for 8 hours a day for my board exam.

During these times, I would find it beneficial to take the properly prescribed medication from a licensed physician. Taking the medication dramatically reduced my drive for creativity, discovery and invention. I was then able to be content to sit and complete my studying without even thinking about my book for most of the day. My drive to invent was lowered and I was then satisfied with the act of replication (monotonous studying).

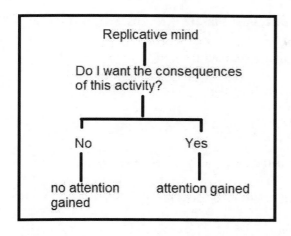

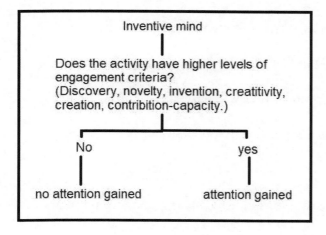

It is this algorithm which is part of the very reason that I chose the name "inventive" when trying to describe the mind-type of a person with ADHD. Their mind is driven to discover, much like the mind of an inventor. The replicative mind is driven by the known consequences of activities (pre-frontal cortex driven behavior).

People with replicative minds must merely ask themselves if they want the known consequences of an action and then they can have sufficient directed attention to complete the task and gain the consequence.

Contrasted to an inventive mind, the consequences of actions are often unknown. That is what makes it "discovery." Their intelligence is directed towards an action with unknown consequences. They are driven into the darkness of the unknown, to find whatever is there and bring it to light. Whether this means to create or invent something, or to merely see what will happen, or to understand something which was not previously understood.

The replicative mind seeks the known consequence and the inventive minds seeks the unknown consequence. This is a major hallmark of the inventive mind and perhaps the main feature of what sets it apart from replicative minds.

5. The Inventive Mind is Problem-Based

I have spent a lot of time trying to figure out the difference between people with ADHD and people without ADHD. What is it that gets me to pay attention vs. what gets people without ADHD to pay attention? There are a lot of factors to answering this question. Frankly, that is why this book has more than one chapter.

Through lots of introspection and experience sitting in classes listening to people lecture, I figured something out: My brain works backwards. I need the problem first and the lecture second. When someone stands up in front of me and starts lecturing, I feel like my brain is just kind of waiting to engage. What is it waiting for? A problem!

This may seem a bit odd to most people. It seems strange to give someone a problem when they don't have the skills or information necessary to solve it yet. It makes a lot more sense to teach someone the skills and knowledge to solve problems before you give them a problem, because they won't be able to solve the problem that you give them until they are taught how. Regardless of whether it makes sense, the ADHD brain needs to have the problem first. Imagine it like the bird. It flies through the air, until it sees the school of fish. THEN it dives. Dolphins are already submerged in the water to begin with. They don't need to see fish in order to be motivated to get wet because they are already wet to begin with. Birds are different.

Solution First   **Problem First**

When you give the solution first (the lecture) to an inventive mind, it's kind of like giving away the end of the story. It's like telling their brain "there is nothing to be discovered here so move along." What is the point of watching a story when you already know how it's going to end? It's like handing a map of the world to someone who wants to be an explorer. It takes the wind out of their sails and the motivation out of their minds.

The inventive mind daydreams until it hits its head up against a wall it can't get around. The problem is their motivation. It is their reason to dive in headfirst. You need to give the inventor some time to try solving the problem so that his mind knows what questions it is seeking answers to. It needs a mission to discover. I have found that, for some reason, my mind tends to think that it can figure everything out and that I don't need lectures. Even when I logically know that I really do need lectures to learn, there must be some part of my mind that won't accept that I need lectures in order to learn. This part of my brain must be preventing me from paying attention.

It's kind of childish really. My brain, by default, assumes that I can figure anything out and so I don't have to listen to this person talking. I zone out to a daydream until my brain realizes I, indeed, don't know how to do something. I remember thinking this way when I was kid. I recall someone doing a magic trick. I watched the trick and was bored because I thought I could easily do it. "I can do that" I said. "Oh really? Here try," they replied. I was handed the instruments for the magic trick and after several failed attempts I realized that I could not reproduce the trick. Suddenly I was engaged and no longer bored. My brain needs to be shown that it is lacking something before it will go and seek for it. When I try to teach my daughter with ADHD, she often says "I already know how to do that", I reply with, "Okay, then show me." She discovers that she cannot do what I am trying to teach her and suddenly she is teachable.

I used to get story problems as well as normal problems on my math exams. I would do significantly better on the story problems because my mind got engaged to try and solve the persons dilemma. Not only that, but I could visualize the actual parts of the problem better when they were described. The inventive mind needs a quest, or a goal or an objective. It needs some kind of motivation to learn or else it will not learn.

The most important question that must be answered for an inventive

mind is "why?" This question must be answered before any real

learning can occur.

The ADHD mind has an active posterior cingulate gyrus. This is

interactive with the dorsal attention network, which is involved in

visual attention and eye movement related to "top down processing."

It is also involved with the frontoparietal control network which has to do with executive motor control. The posterior cingulate gyrus seems to activate during visual tasks involved with incentives, making it a motivation related part of the brain. Perhaps now you can see a little clearer why people who have been diagnosed with ADHD seem to need to work with their hands, and images and to have a clear motive before they can learn something.

The very thing which drives a replicative mind to success is the contentment to replicate the same behaviors with an expected predictable outcome. That makes them successful. This driving motive is lacking in an inventive mind, which deters them from monotony and predictable outcomes. Instead they are lured toward the unknown, to the outside of the box, and to pursuits with unsure outcomes with incentive-based motivation (they will get some kind of reward if they create or discover something good). This is the perfect brain chemistry for an inventor.

Understanding this is vital to teaching them. Inventive minds are geared towards discovering solutions to problems with some kind of incentive-based motivation. This means that you have to present them with the problem that they are unable to solve. Once the problem is demonstrated and the inventive mind realizes it cannot solve the problem, it becomes activated with motivation to learn and gain the skill to find a solution.

It is actually a good idea for inventive minds to be given the problem along with some time so that they can fail in their attempt to solve it before you even try to teach them anything at all. This approach would frustrate most people, but it is what really kicks the inventive mind into gear. They won't care what you are talking about until they know they are absolutely certain that they can't solve it without assistance. THEN they will want to discover what you know and want to listen to you. The inventive mind doesn't find something interesting unless it realizes that it needs to discover it in order to solve a problem. The failure to provide a solution answers that important question of "why." Once you fail at something, you know why learning about it is important. Now that this question is answered, learning begins.

I bought a shed to store my tools in. I picked up and read the instructions included with the shed… just kidding. I left the stupid instructions in the box! I could put this thing together without instructions! At least I thought I could. My brain had to hit its head against the wall a few times trying to do it without the instructions. Usually, I am fairly proficient at putting things together without ever looking at instructions. It wasn't until I had tried several times and failed to put the shed together successfully that I had any inclination to even crack the instruction booklet open (and thankfully I had my brother-in-law there to read it for me... I HATE instruction manuals). I know how my mind works and I know that reading the instruction manual is pretty much impossible until I have exhausted all attempts to figure things out on my own. My brain can't seem to visualize what it is even trying to do until I have tried to do it for a while and failed. If there are pictures in the instruction manual, I can do much better with images. I think it is because it involves spatial learning.

The current replicative education system first demonstrates the information and then asks the questions in the form of homework or a test. The students with inventive minds are not given the problems yet and so will have extreme difficulty paying attention to a lesson because they don't know what they are going to need the information for or their minds assume that they already know it. They sit in class daydreaming with no motive to learn until they go home. Then they open up the homework and try to do a problem. At the end of the day, they are starting where they should have started at the beginning of the day. For their mind, the lecture was pointless information because the inventive mind does not synchronize with the pre-frontal cortex to make the connection to the "point." The point being that learning this information will be helpful tonight when you want to try to do your homework. It won't make this connection until the problem, and therefore motivation, are presented before them.

You obviously aren't going to be able to solve the problem when it is given first because you haven't learned anything yet. This "failure-first" model is what promotes "learning-second" behavior. Primary failure is your friend. Once people with inventive minds fail, then you can teach them, and you will see how much more receptive they are. Then and only then can you have a more effective time teaching the inventive mind because now the inventive mind recognizes that there are problems that need solving. The very thing that drives the inventive mind away from monotony, the need to discover, is the very thing that drives it toward invention and is also the thing that deters it from listening in replicative class environments.

Here is how teaching could be effectively formatted for a person with inventive minds:

Teaching method for an Inventive mind

1. **INTRO**: A very short explanation of what the lecture and problem will cover.

2. **PROBLEM**: Exposure to a problem (what they should be able to solve at the end of the lecture).

3. **DISCOVER**: Some time given to discover that the problem cannot be solved currently.

3. **TEACH**: Short lecture that explains how to solve the problem.

4. **SOLVE**: Another opportunity to solve the problem given earlier.

5. **REPEAT**: Then back to stage one.

This model would work well for something that involves math or other problem solving.

Subjects which are essentially memorizing, such as history or psychology, need to be approached with a different format. I will explain this other format in the next chapter.

It seems like inventive minds are at quite a disadvantage since classrooms are not set up with a format that is compatible for them. So if we have ADHD, and want to do well in school, what do we do? We can cry about it. We can give up and drop out of school. Obviously, neither of these options are helpful at achieving our goals. Are we at a disadvantage? Yep, we simply don't learn things which have already been discovered by other people as well as replicative minds do. "Discovering" things that have already been discovered just isn't our thing... that's more of a replicative thing. If we were extremely proficient at doing things like everyone else, we wouldn't be driven to try new ways of doing things; we wouldn't be driven to explore and discover. If we were excellent at replicating, we wouldn't be as motivated to try and invent. If we could find immediate and easy success in replicating other people's methods, we wouldn't get our hands dirty finding new ways to do things. It is our particular brain make-up that promotes creativity, uniqueness, discovery, and invention. It is also our specific brain make-up which makes it much harder for us in the classroom and on with tests. The wings of the bird make it better equipped to fly, but poorly equip it for easy swimming.

As hard as it may be for us to replicate, we need to learn all that has been done. In order to invent we must push ourselves to the edge of all that is known in order to take that step out into the unknown. We are almost useless to invent until we have learned all that can be learned. We need to learn how others have done things first. Asking an inventive mind to do things the way that other people do things is probably about as hard as asking a replicative mind to do things in a way that has never been done before. It just goes against the grain. Once we have gone to the edge of technology, we can apply our minds, which are perfectly designed for discovery, to think outside the box and come up with new ways to do things and push the limits of what people thought was possible. It will likely take you longer to replicate, but DO NOT GIVE UP. It will come eventually. If you can follow the full ADHD Learning Model in the last chapter, it should go faster and be much easier.

If you are an adult and want to be successful, try to figure out why you need to know the information before you try to learn it. You may find it helpful to take a moment before each lecture and really try to connect your purpose to your studies and really focus on your motivation before each study session. Then organize the material that you need to learn into small bite size chunks, and, if possible, create a learning objective for each section. It could even be something like: "I want to be able to solve problems that look like this (insert sample problem here).

Having some kind of motivation that you are aiming for can help your brain to retain what you are trying to learn. Putting the motivation in front of you while you are studying can help you to exogenously produce the connection that would normally be made by the pre-frontal cortex. Thus, allowing you to have motivation to complete your tasks.

It might be a good idea to try a few practice questions before you read a chapter or lecture so you know what you are up against. Unless you can induce a hyper-focused state, you are going to need more exposure than most everyone else because your mind isn't as adhesive when it comes to replication. But by first exposing yourself to problems, you can put some glue on the learning materials and get them to stick in a problem-based kind of way.

6. The Inventive Mind is Project-Based

I remember walking into class one day in the 9th grade and my teacher announcing that today was the day for me to give my presentation. I had no idea that people were even giving presentations (I must have been daydreaming as usual). I didn't want to fail so I asked someone what my presentation was supposed to be on. They pointed to the pages in the book that I was supposed to give the report on that day, as they were listed on a piece of paper that I did not recall ever seeing before. I opened the book to the pages and started to read. I got about 2 minutes in when my name was called to go to the front of the classroom and give my presentation.

Now to some of you, this may sound like a nightmare. But for me, this was every day life. I never knew when something was due, or what it was that as due, or even that something was due in the first place. I would find out on the spot and so I had to get very good at figuring things out and performing on a moment's notice. This was just another one of those days.

When I got to the front of the classroom, I acted confident so the teacher wouldn't know that I was totally unprepared. My eyes shifted to the bold words in the text book. I addressed each one of them and gave descriptions of each one and then came up with some examples on the spot. I managed to get an A on that particular assignment, which was good because I had failed so many other assignments and tests that I needed a good score to raise my average to my usual grade of a C.

These kinds of survival tactics are how I passed high school with a C average. I never knew what was due or when it was due so I relied on classmates to tell me what the homework was. If I had understood and applied the ADHD Learning Model then, it would have been much easier for me to get A's and I wouldn't have had to always be scrambling for survival.

When I was in college, my wife would tell me when assignments were due. This helped me so much and is a big part of why I did so well in undergraduate school. When I started taking premedical classes I no longer had my wife to rely on. This meant that I had to find out a way to figure out when things were due by myself. I created an excel spreadsheet that I looked at daily. It had a list of all of my assignments and when they were due.

When I became more organized it helped me survive. But it also did other things for me. Having a list of my assignments helped my homework become project-based and goal-oriented. Inventive minds can have a hard time keeping track of goals so it is essential that they

Inventive minds are project-based

have a place where they can reference them frequently or else they are unlikely to ever accomplish them.

The Inventive (ADHD) mind has less synchronous communication between the pre-frontal cortex and the posterior cingulate gyrus. This means that their behavior is more difficult to connect to a desired consequence. So where a replicative mind may go to work every day in order to get a paycheck, an inventive mind does not make the connection between the activity and the pay check very well. Yes, they understand that the behavior will earn them a paycheck at the end of the day, it's just that knowing this does not make the behavior as rewarding for an inventive mind as it does for a replicative mind. All because of the lack of synchronous communication in the brain regions.

With the lacking consequence-driven rewards coming from the prefrontal cortex, the inventive mind is driven by other motivators. These motivators are found in discovery and accomplishment. This is one reason that video games may be so engaging for people with ADHD, because video games are full of discovery and have such rapid consequences.

"Project-based" means that the learning has a goal. Achieving this goal provides the needed motivation. This may seem like a

contradiction. In an earlier chapter I explained how the inventive mind doesn't have a very good ability to engage in activities based on a predictable outcome. That is still true. However, I have found that engaging in a project just one time is very doable. Repeating the exact same project to produce the exact same result is much, much less doable. I believe that first-time projects are a form of discovery in and of themselves. A mind only really needs to learn something once, if it learns it well enough. So, a project that is oriented around a learning activity needs to only be done one time. The inventive mind is drawn to do a project because of the discovery that will occur in the process along with several other factors.

What projects offer Inventive minds

1. **Hands-on Interaction** (free-range and spatial learning)

2. **Creation** (see engagement criteria)

3. **Contribtion** opportunity

4. **Interaction**-based learning (if it can be shared)

5. **Discovery** (projects are full of this)

6. **Novelty** (change is often a requirement for project completion)

7. **Motivation** (completing a project creates a sense of reward)

8. **Deadline** opportunities (needed for timely completion)

If you can combine the discovery project to learning something then you achieve your goal of learning. Since the inventive mind can have a hard time hanging on to the project if any parts become monotonous (most projects have these kinds of parts), it is very good for the project to be short.

It is also a good idea to have the project mapped out on a calendar and broken down into small attainable goals. If the project is not approached this way then failing to complete the project is very likely. Inventive minds are notorious for not finishing projects because nearly all projects have monotonous parts to them which strongly deters active engagement for the inventive mind. But if the inventive mind can have their goals on a calendar in front of them, it's like a way of exogenously giving the inventive mind motivation that a replicative mind naturally already has because of their pre-frontal cortex synchrony.

As I stated earlier, in order for a behavior to be rewarding for an inventive mind you need to break it up into small projects. Completing the project brings reward to the inventive mind and so they are working towards completing the project. These projects can come in the form of creating a set of flash cards, or coming up with memory exercises, or making a lesson plan. The projects need to be fairly short (this is determined on a case-by-case basis).

Besides being project-based, learning for the inventive mind needs to be goal oriented. The inventive mind is not as readily able to keep the goal of the behavior in sight as a replicative mind, so it is a very good idea to set a specific goal and then have that goal broken down into lots of small project-based goals.

Motivation is Vital for the Inventive Mind

If someone you know is doing poorly in school and/or work it is possible that ADHD isn't the problem at all. It could be an issue of motivation or some other problem. It's a good idea to consult a medical professional about a diagnosis so that you know what the issue is. Then you can begin to deal with it properly.

Before you start going down the ADHD road, make sure that motivation is there. If the individual lacks motivation, then it doesn't matter if you have best learning model ever created.

Success follows motivation. You can have the fastest car in the world, but if you don't step on the gas pedal, you won't get anywhere. You may need to hang the motivation out in front of them, like hanging a carrot on a string in front of a rabbit, if you are trying to teach someone with ADHD. If you are an adult with ADHD, then you may need to put your goal in front of you, perhaps a picture of what you are trying to accomplish placed somewhere so you can see it every day until you achieve your goal.

One of the students in our medical school who got one of the highest board scores almost failed out of grade school when he was younger. He did not have ADHD. His problem was motivation. When he was really young, his teacher tasked him with reading a book by a certain date. He read nearly the entire book, and was on the last few pages when he reached the due date. His teacher gave him an F because he wasn't quite done yet. He was so frustrated because he put in a lot of time and effort into reading that book and got nothing out of it. He felt like his teacher had cheated him and he felt hurt by the bad grade. After that failing grade, he stopped even trying in school. He was upset and hurt and felt cheated and so his "not trying" was his way of getting back into control of his life and getting back at the people who cheated him. He did not have ADHD, but he didn't pay attention in class. This was motivation, not ADHD.

Repeated failure, which is often associated with ADHD, can certainly kill motivation. Imagine what it would feel like if every time you starting trying to learn something, someone got angry at you and put you down. Inventive minds learn by getting their hands on things and talking about things, if they cant get their hands on it and they cant talk about it, then they cant learn about it properly. Classrooms designed for replicative minds do not allow enough discussion and they do not allow you to get up out of your chair and discover things with your hands. These environments are almost perfectly designed to suck the motivation right out of a person with an inventive mind.

Then imagine if every test you ever took was about how to eat ham (I tried to think of a boring or non-relevant subject). To an inventive mind every subject is boring and non-relevant until they see that it is relevant. The relevance and importance of a subject is often NEVER explained, and if it is, then it is often at the end of the lecture.

How most people learn

The only way someone with ADHD can effectively learn

The inventive mind needs to be engaged first, then taught. This engagement triggers motivation and drive. I used to do much better on the math story problems because I became motivated to find out if cutting this tree down would destroy my house (or whatever problem the story presented to me). Once I saw there was a reason to figure it out, my brain became engaged and I wanted to solve the problem. Until you engage the inventive mind with motivation, every word out of your mouth might as well be, "this is how you eat ham."

It is the constant boredom often associated with ADHD that frequently kills motivation. Inventive minds need a problem, they need a project, they need to get their hands on it (they need to try it out), they need to be able to talk about it. If they can't do these things, then they can't learn and discover.

If the inventive mind has been submerged for a while in the current school system they may have already developed a lack of motivation as they have the hunger for discovery drained from their hearts and minds. If this has happened, then when you put material in front of them in the ADHD format, they may not have the motivation to even give it a try and if they do, they may not care anymore.

Replicative environments can literally prevent inventive minds from learning. How many years passed before you started getting angry and defiant at people not letting you learn anything? I hinted at this earlier, but I really think that the development of Oppositional Defiant Disorder may be a totally reasonable response from the perspective of a child with ADHD. In order for you to understand, imagine yourself as a child being repeatedly disciplined (people yelling at you, putting you down, punishing you), because you were told to pick up a car and you couldn't do it, but you tried really hard. They demanded you to do it and expected you to and as much as you tried, you were unable. You are then labeled as a bad kid. Is it any wonder that so many kids with ADHD end up in prison? They learn from an early age that authority figures make demands that are impossible and they learn that people think they are bad kids.

Before shoving some new thing in front of a person with ADHD, you really need to manage their motivation first. My motivation to get an education faded as my self confidence eroded. For me, education was just another way to be told over and over than I wasn't as bright as the other kids. It was just another way to be told that I couldn't do what other people could do and that I had to let go of my dreams and ambitions because I wasn't good enough to ever achieve anything. It wasn't until I had gone through four years of college that I started having some confidence to rekindle my dreams.

If an inventive mind has no motivation it cannot thrive. Motivation comes in the form of hope, self-confidence, and believing that they can be successful. They have to believe that something good will come from their efforts. They need to visualize the good thing and to visualize themselves achieving it. Those things can rekindle the spark of discovery, creativity, and that drive to learn.

Remember that many inventive minds are motivated to learn through discovery with trial and error. It's frustrating sometimes when you want to just show them how to do something (replicate your behavior), but let them have an opportunity to discover and fail a few times and then their brains may be primed and motivated to watch you do it the right way.

The issue becomes getting the inventive mind focused on the motivation of the task at hand. I struggle with this every day. I know I should be studying for my upcoming test, but I want to go online and learn more about the function of the posterior cingulate gyrus, and I want to work on my books, or write a blog post, or build something.

You can fuel the motivation by having their goals and their projects all on a list in front of them with small boxes to check it off. This can help to get the inventive mind more synchronous with their desired outcome (since their minds are not always synchronous with the prefrontal cortex where that kind of process normally occurs).

Deadlines for the inventive mind

Having a deadline is essential. I have a friend who was diagnosed with ADHD who tells me, "I do my best work when I have my back against the wall." What he means is that when he is cornered (pinned into a corner by a deadline), his mind goes into hyper-focus (it becomes extremely motivated) and he is able to do whatever he set out to accomplish. Deadlines are like pressing down on the gas pedal of our minds.

The deadlines do not need to be external in nature. They can be self-imposed. Deadlines are especially good for inventive minds because they can be the motivation for the inventive mind when it cannot find interest in it for the sake of discovery or creativity.

My father builds his boats with a deadline. The deadline is the beginning of the fishing season. Because of this deadline his brain comes into hyper-focus project-mode and he is able to work incredible hours and come up with solutions that would not normally be available to him without the deadline.

When you have something that you would like to accomplish as a person with an inventive mind. **Failing to set a deadline is basically like choosing to never complete the task.** Having the deadline for a project will also help narrow down and sharpen your focus.

One of the main reasons that inventive minds rarely complete their projects is because they lack the deadline and jump from project to project and become so spread out that they make almost no progress on any of their goals. Having a deadline forces the inventive mind into one task. It is only by focusing on one task that you are likely to finish it.

School is actually a wonderful environment for this because schools have exams. The deadline of an exam can help the inventive mind to stay focused. The problem I faced in medical school is that I had about a dozen tests every month. There were so many tests that I would lose track of them. I had too many deadlines. In order to be successful I needed to spend a little bit of time on each subject each day. I would start studying on a subject and if I was lucky, I would hyper-focus, but then before I knew it, the day would be over and I had failed to review the material on the other subjects. Failing to review material is a sure way to forget it. That is why scheduling your day is so important in conjunction with the deadline.

Do inventive minds really have an attention deficit?

ADHD stands for Attention Deficit Hyperactive Disorder. Is the "Attention Deficit" part really accurate? Well, most people would say so. And its true, most of the time we do struggle to pay attention to things that do not grab our interest. But inventive minds also experience something I've mentioned several times, called "hyper-focus." It's what happens when we are paying attention to something that we are very interested in. A few moments ago I was helping my daughter with her homework. She was supposed to color something that began with "E" as part of her homework. My daughter, who has an incredibly inventive mind, hyper-focused on this particular activity. She dug around in the colored pencil bin until she found exactly the shade of gray she wanted and then she carefully colored the elephant. She found a shade of pink for the inside of the elephants ears and then colored the elephants toenails. To top it off she elaborated the elephant and gave it something she called an "ancient hat" that was tall and had stripes. Pretty elaborate for a five-year old. The frustrating part is that I wanted her to focus on the next problem, rather than taking a century coloring her "ancient hat," but her inventive mind was busy creating and discovering things that she found interesting.

She has an attention deficit for things that are not engaging or interesting for her. But she does not have an attention deficit for activities that she finds amusing or fascinating. Usually these activities involve creativity.

This very book is another example of the hyper-focus. I wrote most of this book in about 2 weeks while working full time at medical rotations, studying in the morning for my shelf exam, and also being a dad and husband. But every spare moment I could possibly get a sentence in, I was typing. My mind became super engaged in creating this project and seeing it to completion.

My dad is the same way with his boats. For months and years at a time, all he can think about is his latest project. He dreams about it. When he wakes up, he immediately starts revamping the newest aspect of the project he is working on. Just the other day (he is 70 years old now), he created a new adaption to his boat that allows him to elongate the deck space on a boat he made last year.

This is the drive of an inventive mind. They become obsessed with their projects. The DSM-V even said, that people with ADHD act as if they are "driven with a motor." It's almost like their brain is constantly searching and scanning their environment for something to discover with their hands. Once they find it, they learn by inspecting it kinesthetically. They come up with creative adaptions outside of the box. Their brain is resistant to learning things the same way as everyone else learns things. They are repulsed by instruction manuals (which is what teaches you how to do things in traditional ways). Maybe this resistance is what helps them to think differently and approach things in new ways.

The problem really isn't so much a deficit of attention as it is a deficit of attention to things that are not interesting to them. I have tried to figure out what makes something interesting to the ADHD mind. I have noticed that it frequently has to fill a few criteria. It usually has some creative aspect to it, whether socially or physically. It often has to be part of a project or something that can become their own project. They need to have free range to explore a subject on their terms. They usually have to see themselves doing something with it in a way that will benefit themselves or others in some way.

So how does this help you with your (or your child's) schooling? If you want your mind to kick into hyper-focus mode, then try to turn your homework into presentations or projects. To learn in medical school, I found that preparing a YouTube presentation was especially helpful. I would gather images and draw examples, then come up with a logical order to explain the material. When I was done, I would have a powerpoint presentation or a whiteboard full of drawings and writing. Then I would present this information to YouTube. Turning my studies into a video project made all the difference for me.

Other times I would make it into a project by creating as many questions from the material as I could. I would fill the page with questions and answers. Other times I would make flash cards. The time would fly by as I was putting the project together in hyper-focus mode. I was making something to benefit myself or others. I had free reign over the project. It had creative aspects to it. All of the criteria were met for hyper-focus to occur.

7. The Inventive Mind is Interaction-Based

When I was in grade school I tried to do my homework alone. It was very hard for me to stay focused on my homework. I would try and try, but get nowhere. When I did force myself to read, I would finish a page and have no idea what I just read. It was like the information just slid off of my brain and landed on the floor.

Before I was married, I took a few college classes. I had mediocre results. It was definitely better than grade school, but I just still struggled to get through the material and have it stick.

Then after I was married I went to college with my wife. We took our classes together. We studied together and talked about the material together. We quizzed each other and had some kind of social relationship around the material we studied together. Suddenly I started getting A's. Like straight A's.

None of our classes required much more than reading comprehension (degrees in psychology are that way). A great way to get reading comprehension for an ADHD is to talk about the subject matter, a lot. That is exactly what my wife and I did. For those kinds of classes, that was the perfect solution.

My wife and I unknowingly created an ideal learning environment for a person with ADHD and that is why I was able to excel and get good enough grades to get into medical school. Once my wife graduated and we had our first born, she was no longer my study partner. I had started to pursue medicine and had to take classes without her. I tried to find study partners that I could replicate the same kind of learning environment that I had with my wife. Fortunately for me, many of my classes had students in them that were willing to create that learning environment, but in a few of my classes I couldn't find anyone willing.

I struggled a lot in those classes. I saw my first C grades on my undergraduate school transcript during this time. Also, most of the pre-med classes were not mere reading comprehension based. They involved lots of memorization and very a large degree of problem solving. Just reading and talking about the material isn't enough for pre-med or med classes.

As I have stated many times, the inventive (ADHD) mind is easily bored with monotony. It requires higher levels of stimulation in order to keep attention and interest (probably why they do so well with intense movies and video games). Social interaction can give that needed level of stimulation and breaks up the monotony. Plus it gives the inventive mind a chance to verbally express what has been learned. This type of autobiographical (self spoken) way of learning is more compatible with ADHD learning and is much more easily retained in memory with easier recall.

An ideal social learning environment is as follows:

1. The student understands that they are going to be teaching the information that they are about to learn.

2. They are presented with the information. It should be a short piece of information. The length should depend upon what the person feels they can handle.

3. The information is then organized and broken down into an outline with teaching points and questions in a lesson format.

4. Then the information is presented orally and on visually on a white-board or a piece of paper.

Why is this effective?

1. The inventive ADHD mind was given a "Problem": This information needs to be taught.

2. The problem was "project-based." It had a clear beginning and ending point that was reasonable in length of time (achievement was not too far to grasp).

3. The activity required the student to condense the information into note form, thus categorizing and condensing the information for memory storage and utilizing spatial memory on the page in front of them.

4. The information was then presented orally, which dramatically increases information retention.

5. The information presented was drawn on the white-board, utilizing spatial memory (where bits of information were written on the white board will aid in retrieval of the data because it existed somewhere in space outside of their mind).

If the student does not have another student to teach to in that moment, they can record the lecture with an understanding that the lecture will be viewed by someone later.

Medical school is an academic environment unlike any other I had ever encountered. I was being bombarded with more information in a week than I had been presented with in a year in undergraduate school. I tried to recreate the ideal group-learning environment, but people were so stressed and hard-pressed to study silently that I couldn't find anyone to recreate the ADHD Learning Model environment that helped me excel in undergraduate school.

I could find people to "study with", but they usually wanted to just study in the same room as me, with the occasional bit of conversation or interaction with the material. I tried this, but it simply did not work. If anything, it lessened my effectiveness because I had someone interesting to talk to. Talking to someone was far more interesting than sitting and reading all day.

I failed test after test. I did so poorly that I was terrified of completely failing out of med school. It was this very harsh learning environment that really pushed me to coming up with the ADHD Learning Model. When I was in medical school, I eventually found some people to study with (and not just "study next to") which is what enabled me to start getting some B's on tests. The study partners were very helpful, but they weren't available for as much time as I would have preferred. I utilized a large variety of methods

Interactive Learning Environments

One-sided interaction. Low engagement.
Not ideal for ADHD Learning Model.

Two-sided interaction. High engagement.
Ideal for ADHD Learning Model.

and tools to engage my ADHD brain, and I passed. In the process the ADHD Learning Model was created.

One thing I discovered, my ADHD mind learns best when I am the one doing the talking. People have their own studying to do and don't always want to sit around and listen to one person talk, but unless I am the one person talking, I am not learning optimally. This means that the optimal group size is two people. That way you don't have to split the "talking time" more than 50%, since talking time is "learning time."

In my experience for most situations study groups are best at two and should never exceed four people unless most of the group members are wanting to sit around and listen to the person with the inventive mind and not do any talking. You see, inventive minds learn and memorize things while they are speaking.

The person with an inventive mind should take the material and then organize it into a lesson. This allows the material to become project-based. The project component is likely to trigger the "hyper-focus" aspect of their inventive mind. They should come up with memorization exercises, outlines, flash cards, questions, and pictures. Then they should teach the lesson that they have prepared.

Then the other group participant should do the same and also share their material. Then the two group participants should go back and do the same thing again with the next piece of material. This should be repeated until all of the material has been learned.

The other nice thing about this is that it creates a deadline when a group member says, "See you at 3 pm to share your presentation on this material."

8. The ADHD Learning Model

You survived reading the ramblings of a person with ADHD. You made it to the most important part of the book. The actual ADHD Learning Model. I will lay out exactly what you need to do.

Part One: Get Ridiculously Organized!

If you have ADHD, you are likely have a strong tendency to be very disorganized and that is the first obstacle to overcome. Don't just get your day organized, but get your whole life organized.

Failing to plan is planning to fail. Since you don't have synchronous communication to your pre-frontal cortex, you need to create a pre-frontal cortex on excel or a calendar. Otherwise you will lose motivation and fail. If you make a plan, then you are on track for success! A life plan is good because it puts everything in your life in context. It also creates the deadline motivation. A life plan helps you prioritize your projects.

Example of Life Plan

year	job	location	Richard	McKenna	Liam	Brielle	Lydia	Clara	Kathryn	Event	vacation
2017	3rd yr	Caldwell	35	31	8	6	4	2	0	Pass all boards, Write the inventive mind	
2018	4th year	Caldwell	36	32	9	7	5	3	1	Graduate from Medical school, get psychiatry residency	
2019	residency 1	Residency	37	33	10	8	6	4	2	Write book title: "Why people hate you"	
2020	residency 2	Residency	38	34	11	9	7	5	3	Write next book idea on same genre	
2021	residency 3	Residency	39	35	12	10	8	6	4	Write the next book idea, same genre	
2022	Residency 4	Residency	40	36	13	11	9	7	5	move to rexburg and start up psychiatry practice	
2023	Psychiatrist near family		41	37	14	12	10	8	6	write my book Mythan	Hawaii
2024	Psychiatrist near family		42	38	15	13	11	9	7	design board game	
2025	Psychiatrist near family		43	39	16	14	12	10	8	invest in a house	Alaska
2026	Psychiatrist near family		44	40	17	15	13	11	9	learn to build log cabins	
2027	Psychiatrist near family		45	41	18	16	14	12	10	1st kid out of the house	Europe
2028	Psychiatrist near family		46	42	19	17	15	13	11	invest in second house	
2029	Psychiatrist near family		47	43	20	18	16	14	12	write "the truth process"	some other place
2030	Psychiatrist near family		48	44	21	19	17	15	13	write "An autobiography by Richard William Wadsworth"	
2031	Psychiatrist near family		49	45	22	20	18	16	14	invest in 3rd house	new place
2032	Psychiatrist near family		50	46	23	21	19	17	15		
2033	Psychiatrist near family		51	47	24	22	20	18	16		new place
2034	Psychiatrist near family		52	48	25	23	21	19	17	invest in fourth house	
2035	Psychiatrist near family		53	49	26	24	22	20	18		new place
2036	Psychiatrist near family		54	50	27	25	23	21	19		
2037	Psychiatrist near family		55	51	28	26	24	22	20	invest in fifth house	new place
2038	Psychiatrist near family		56	52	29	27	25	23	21		
2039	Psychiatrist near family		57	53	30	28	26	24	22		new place
2040	Psychiatrist near family		58	54	31	29	27	25	23	invest in 6th house	
2041	Psychiatrist near family		59	55	32	30	28	26	24	last kid out of the house	new place
2042	Psychiatrist dream location		60	56	33	31	29	27	25		
2043	Psychiatrist dream location		61	57	34	32	30	28	26	invest in 7th house	new place
2044	Psychiatrist dream location		62	58	35	33	31	29	27		
2045	Psychiatrist dream location		63	59	36	34	32	30	28		new place
2046	Psychiatrist dream location		64	60	37	35	33	31	29	invest in 8th house	
2047	retired	dream location	65	61	38	36	34	32	30	Retirement	new place

Figure out what you want to achieve in your life and map it out.

Figure out how old you will be, factor in your family, and plan everything big you want to do.

Now that you have your life organized. Identify your next main goal.

My next main goal (besides completing this book) is to pass my board exams. I got CRAZY organized about exactly what I am going to study and on which days. Then when I am going to review it again. You cant see, but its color coded.

Specific Monthly Goal Plan

I hold my self accountable and I know when I am going to be taking step two of the boards and what I have to do before that date. I have determined how many lectures I need to do a day in order to be done by then.

During medical school I quickly realized that I needed to do even more than just having the week planned out. I needed to have the day scheduled out as well. Hour by hour. I put it into Google Calendar and marked how long I would study for each lecture. Otherwise, I would hyper-focus on one lecture and totally neglect the others, or I would daydream, or get side-tracked and not realize how long I was side-tracked. I would update my Google Calendar every 30 minutes with a report of what I did 30 minutes prior.

Daily 30 Minute Task Plan

In order to succeed, I had to compensate for my differences by getting ridiculously organized. Here is an example of my study schedule for the upcoming test.

Day	Date	Videos, Cards, Questions					Videos					Cards					Questions							Diff
Monday	8-May	1	2	3	4	5																1	2	4
Tuesday	9-May	6	7	8	9	10	1	2	3	4	5											3	4	8
Wednesday	10-May	11	12	13	14	15	6	7	8	9	10											5	6	12
Thursday	11-May	16	17	18	19	20	11	12	13	14	15											7	8	16
Friday	12-May	21	22	23	24	25	16	17	18	19	20											9	10	20
Saturday	13-May																							
Sunday	14-May	Videos, Cards, Questions					Videos					Cards					Questions							
Monday	15-May	26	27	28	29	30	21	22	23	24	25	1	2	3	4	5						11	12	24
Tuesday	16-May	31	32	33	34	35	26	27	28	29	30	6	7	8	9	10						13	14	28
Wednesday	17-May	36	37	38	39	40	31	32	33	34	35	11	12	13	14	15						15	16	32
Thursday	18-May	41	42	43	44	45	36	37	38	39	40	16	17	18	19	20						17	18	36
Friday	19-May	46	47	48	49	50	41	42	43	44	45	21	22	23	24	25						19	20	40
Saturday	20-May																							
Sunday	21-May	Videos, Cards, Questions					Videos					Cards					Questions							
Monday	22-May	51	52	53	54	55	46	47	48	49	50	26	27	28	29	30	1	2	3	4	5	21	22	44
Tuesday	23-May	56	57	58	59	60	51	52	53	54	55	31	32	33	34	35	6	7	8	9	10	23	24	48
Wednesday	24-May	61	62	63	64	65	56	57	58	59	60	36	37	38	39	40	11	12	13	14	15	25	26	52
Thursday	25-May	66	67	68	69	70	61	62	63	64	65	41	42	43	44	45	16	17	18	19	20	27	28	56
Friday	26-May	71	72	73	74	75	66	67	68	69	70	46	47	48	49	50	21	22	23	24	25	29	30	60
Saturday	27-May																							
Sunday	28-May	Videos, Cards, Questions					Videos					Cards					Questions							
Monday	29-May	76	77	78	79	80	71	72	73	74	75	51	52	53	54	55	26	27	28	29	30	31	32	64
Tuesday	30-May	81	82	83	84	85	76	77	78	79	80	56	57	58	59	60	31	32	33	34	35	33	34	68
Wednesday	31-May	86	87	88	89	90	81	82	83	84	85	61	62	63	64	65	36	37	38	39	40	35	36	72
Thursday	1-Jun	91	92	93	94	95	86	87	88	89	90	66	67	68	69	70	41	42	43	44	45	37	1	76
Friday	2-Jun	96	97	98	99	100	91	92	93	94	95	71	72	73	74	75	46	47	48	49	50	2	3	80
Saturday	3-Jun																							
Sunday	4-Jun	Videos, Cards, Questions					Videos					Cards					Questions							

I was first given this idea of keeping a study journal by my chemistry professor in undergraduate school. He told us to keep track of how long we spent studying because people didn't spend as much time studying as they thought they did. I used Google Calendar as a method of not only planning out my day, but also keeping myself accountable. If I got distracted on Facebook or YouTube, I would have to block out that time on Google Calendars as "Facebook" instead of studying for biochemistry, as I had originally planned.

I would insert the times into my spreadsheet and total them for the day (the image I show above is a different method of keeping track of my studies than the one I am describing now). When I first started doing this I literally was disturbed at how much time I spent on social media and how little time I spent on my studies. I thought I was spending twelve hours studying, but in reality it was like seven. Once I was keeping close track of my time, I was able to hit the twelve hours and had better control of where my attention was spent because I was holding myself accountable to the schedule.

By way of summary, if you get organized, it helps in several ways: First it helps you know what you have to accomplish. This helps you stay goal oriented which is a big deal for people with inventive minds because we tend to easily lose track of the goal because our posterior cingulate gyrus does not have very good synchronous communication with our prefrontal cortex (the part of our brain that helps us make decisions with the end goal in mind).

Second, it helps you stay on track. We tend to get side tracked easily because we are so motivated by novelty and discovery. When we find something interesting, we are drawn towards it. Video games, youtube and facebook can be our undoing if we do not keep meticulous watch over our time and how we are spending it. Five minutes can turn into five hours in the blink of an eye if we hyper-focus on something other than our homework.

Third, it compensates for our tendency to not complete tasks. When a task gets boring or monotonous, we tend to move onto another task that offers us the discovery that our brains are searching for. Unless we learn to finish projects, we will struggle to find success. Getting organized and setting time-based goals is a great way to overcome this obstacle to our success.

WARNING!!! Make sure that you plan for recreation, sleep and exercise. If you do not put adequate time in for these activities then your performance will diminish and you may end up getting depressed and doing poorly. Cutting on sleep is never worth it. Cutting out exercise and recreation is bad for performance. You need to treat this like a marathon and not a sprint or else you will get gassed and end up not reaching your goal.

Part Two: Gather Information About the Class

Different types of classes require different learning styles. Some classes require good reading comprehension (history and psychology). Other classes require very detailed memorization (pharmacology, anatomy and biology). Yet other classes require specific problem solving skills (Math and Chemistry). Depending on the type of class it is you will need to utilize different methods.

In order to find out what kind of class it is, you may need to talk to other students who have taken the class and done well. Get as much information as you can. Ask them for tips. Ask them how they studied. Ask what the tests were like. This is so vital. You can waste a lot of time trying to study the wrong things in the wrong way. You will get better at getting information about classes as you take more classes.

PART THREE: FIND A STUDY PARTNER OR GROUP

I cannot stress how important this is. If you are able to do one thing, this may be it. Hopefully you can find success here. Sometimes this can be the hardest part of all. You need to find a group or study partner that is going to permit a type of group study that involves several important aspects:

1. The material should be divided up between the members and they should teach each other

2. The group should quiz each other on high yield points for each subject division

3. The group should be able to meet daily (or as frequently as possible).

4. Give each other deadlines "we will meet at this time and present this information."

Things to avoid:

1. BE CAREFUL ABOUT TALKING OFF TOPIC. This kills group effectiveness. People who break this rule should be threatened to be expelled from the group. A tiny bit of talking is okay, but if you have someone who just doesn't know when to quit and wont stop, you may have to give them the boot.

2. Studying next to each other is not the same thing as studying WITH each other. Replicative minds do well studying next to each other.

Alternative: If you absolutely cannot find sufficient study groups, then you can do what I did and create a youtube channel and then practice teaching the computer screen. If you want to see how I did this, feel free to check out my youtube channel

www.youtube.com/channel/UCy4Y8JCwc8hyqO_abw74Teg

Part Four: Identify the Problem (Goal)

When you go to study, you need to take a minute to persuade

yourself why you need to learn whatever it is you are studying. You

may have to take a moment before each study period really

visualizing this. Take yourself into the future and imagine taking the

test. Try to expose yourself to a few sample test questions if possible

so you can visualize the test better. Focus your mind on why you are

taking this class and how it fits into your long-term goals.

You need to convince your brain that you need to know this stuff,

otherwise you are going to lose track of why you need to know this

stuff and when it gets boring you will go on to other activities.

Working to convince your brain also makes your brain more "sticky"

for the material. You may learn what you are studying faster and

require less repetitions to keep it retained.

Sometimes before you even start studying anything for the class, it is

a good idea to just quickly skim through the whole book. Take thirty minutes just looking at pictures and chapter headings. Kind of get a preview of all that you will be learning. This will create an infrastructure in your mind. Once the infrastructure is in place, you just have to fill in the gaps. Each time you start a new chapter, do a quick skim through of what you will study for that chapter the day before. Just looking at it will prime your brain to learn it. Your brain considers things to be important if it sees them multiple times.

Part Five: Create a Review Schedule

One of the biggest mistakes that people make is that they learn something and then fail to review it. Because of this their brain dumps it. This has been a highly studied phenomenon.

How many exposures is necessary?

I have found that getting a quick overview first is best. This kind of primes my brain to what I am going to learn. I look over some of the problems and I take in the key points. Maybe I watch the lecture really quick on double speed. Then the next day, after my mind has had a chance to integrate the new vocabulary and ideas into the rest of my brain while I was sleeping, I can watch the video a second time. This second time I really focus on learning it. If it is a recorded lecture I may pause it many times and write out parts of the lecture and then memorize it. I will memorize it using memorization heuristics (these are little "tricks" to make memorizing easier. For example, drawing a picture or making an acronym). Then I will leave it alone for the rest of the day. The next day, I will do a rapid review, to demonstrate my ability to draw from my memory what I have put in my brain. It is the ability to draw information from your brain that is of greatest importance. Many people practice putting things in their brain, but forget to practice pulling things out of their brains. What is going to help them more on their test?

After that, I would recommend reviewing the study material maybe after two days, and then maybe four days. Then maybe once a week, for a month or so, then once a month for a year. Then after that you may only have to review it once a year. Most of the time the test will be after a few weeks, so you don't even need to think that far out for academic purposes.

The Ideal Study Review Schedule:

1. A quick preview the day before you study it. On day one.

2. A long and in depth learning and memorization period. On day two.

3. A quick preview the next day. On day three.

4. A quick preview the next week. On day seven.

5. A quick preview a week later. On day fourteen.

6. A quick preview a month later. On day thirty.

Part Six: The Act of Learning

Inventive minds tend to have fantastic spatial memories. Spatial memory means that they if they can visualize the material and see it in a more physical way, then it is easier for them to recall it. There are several methods of utilizing this spatial memory.

In history, spatial memory was first recognized as a way of recalling information during the times of ancient Greece. A man had a party with his friends. The friends were sitting at a table eating food when the ceiling collapsed and crushed all of them. When the heavy stone ceiling was removed their bodies were so smashed that they were beyond recognition. The man, the host, closed his eyes and mentally visualized where his friends were sitting at the table. By doing this he was able to identify all of the bodies.

Kind of a gruesome story, but a very effective model of storing information. If you can put information somewhere in space, it is much easier to retrieve. There was a modern Sherlock Holmes TV show that illustrated this kind of memory. In the show, Sherlock called it his "mind palace." He would store information in there and when he wanted to retrieve it, he would go to that place in his mind where it was stored and he would retrieve it.

When I was in medical school, I used to draw a silly picture. The silly picture might be a creature or person that sounded a bit like the name of the medication I was trying to remember. Then I would write down many attributes about this medication. I would store the bits of information onto this silly picture as parts of his body. For example, if the medication had a side effect of osteoporosis, I would draw him with tiny thin bones. If it had a long half life, I might put a clock on his head with the time set to the time of the half life.

Storing the information this way made retrieval MUCH easier.

I found this particularly helpful with microbiology. When I had to

remember the characteristics of a particular microbe, I would make a

list of all of those characteristics and then encode them. When it was

time to recall something, it was as easy as pulling it out of the

drawing. Included with the drawing I would also come up with a

story. The story would also encode bits of information in it. Once I

had the story and the picture made, most of the work was done.

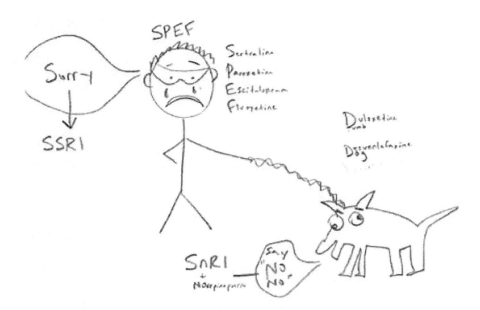

You may observe that trying to memorize my picture is very challenging. I recommend coming up with your own creative pictures. The above picture easily enabled me to memorize a long list of medication names and certain attributes about them, but that was because I was the one who put it all together (btw, do not use the information in the picture above to make medical decisions). Another fantastic trick to memorize lists of information is to take the first letter of each word and make it into something easier to memorize. For example:

Sertraline, Paroxetine, Escitalopram, and Fluoxetine are all selective serotonin reuptake inhibitors, while Desvenlafaxine and Duloxetine are both Serotonin-Norepinephrine Reuptake inhibitors and Bupropion is atypical.

When you first look at that you might think, "Yikes!" But this is actually super easy to learn. We just have to remember how Mr. SPEF was SoRry, he bought his Dumb Dog, who could only Say "No." So he tied him up with an Atypical Rope. Our brains are better equipped. Can you remember that SPEF was SoRry, and that he bought a Dumb Dog that he tied up with a weird rope? If not then draw a picture.

In the picture

SPEF = Sertraline, Paroxetine, Escitalopram, and Fluoxetine.

Sorry = SSRI

Say No = SnRI

Dumb Dog = Duloxetine, and Desvenlafaxine

Weird rope = Atypical bupROPErion

It takes some practice, but I can pop these off because I used these memorization heuristics (exercises). I didn't have to use this kind of stuff in undergraduate school because there wasn't as much information. There is absolutely no way I would have passed medical school without using these kinds of memory tools. If you come up with the heuristic yourself, you are more likely to remember it and it is going to be better at aiding recall.

Part Seven: Eat the Elephant One Bite at a Time

People with inventive minds are notorious for having fifty projects that they started and none that they finished. Why is this? Because nearly every large undertaking will have parts of it that will require a certain amount of monotonous behavior. This monotonous (or boring) "stuff" shuts down the inventive mind due to the lack of discovery and creativity. It requires pre-frontal cortex thinking. Pre-frontal cortex thinking is what motivates behavior based upon the desired outcome. For example, "I will fill out this paperwork so that I can get a paycheck." Since inventive minds do not have efficient synchronous communication between their pre-frontal and posterior cingulate gyrus, they are not likely to have the necessary motivation to complete big projects unless they find ways around insufficient pre-frontal cortex communication.

If you have an inventive mind and want to finish one of your big projects, you need to write down everything that needs to be done on a list. Then take that list and approximate how much time it will take for each task to be done. Put each item on a calendar with a start and finish date for each activity. Put the ultimate completion date of the large project. Processing this information will help activate your pre-frontal cortex and help with some synchronous communication sufficient for you to get the tasks done. You need to have the calendar somewhere that you can see it. Make the mini-projects small enough that you are not too overwhelmed by them.

I am actually employing this technique with this book. Thinking of writing a book with over a hundred pages is a daunting task for someone with ADHD. But I have turned the book into lots of short blog posts. I only have to do a blog post every day. That is not overwhelming at all, but it will get the book (or any project) done in time.

If you want to use this most effectively, then combine it with the memorization heuristics I talked about earlier. Pile as many facts onto the image as you can. For example, the rope could be on fire and smoking. This might help you remember that Buproprion can help with smoking cessation. Also you could remember that SPEF doesn't have a girlfriend because SSRI's cause "bedroom" dysfunction sometimes. These kinds of things just need to be inserted into the picture and they become easy to remember. As a person with ADHD, our minds are more spatial, so we just have to go to the space on the picture to retrieve the information.

Part Eight: Watching Video Lectures and Recordings

I cannot stress the importance of video lectures enough. As a person with ADHD, I find myself daydreaming frequently. In class, when it is in "real-time", daydreaming completely ruins the ability to learn the material. I will suddenly realize that I have been daydreaming, but now I have no idea what the teacher is even talking about anymore because I missed important points. In class the teacher talks SO SLOWLY that I am falling asleep and more apt to daydream.

Problems With Cass Lectures:

1. Daydreaming makes me miss parts of the lecture.
2. The teacher often talks too slowly.
3. I can only watch it once.
4. The environment is usually extremely distracting.
5. I can't pause to take notes and explore a part of the lecture when my mind hyperfocuses.
6. I can't pause to draw something out if I need to engage in spatial learning to get it.

However, with a recorded lecture, I put the speed to double-time. *[handwritten: Running it ~~[crossed out]~~ at double time]*

Putting it on double-time helps me to not get bored and it makes up *[handwritten: Helps keep me focused and gives me extra time to stop and take notes, or go over something I'm not quite clear on several times.]*

for the many times I have to go back or pause. When I realize that I *[handwritten: INSIGHT- ON SOMETHING I'M NOT QUITE CLEAR on else. Sometimes to gain clarity I will repeat a segment]*

have spaced off, I will just go back a few minutes to where I first *[handwritten: several times (taking additional notes as I go).]*

started spacing off. If I don't understand something, I just watch it *[handwritten: The luxury of a rewind button unfortunately isn't]*

again. Sometimes I have to watch it several times. I also write notes *[handwritten: available in a lecture hall. making]*

while I watch. Or I pause the video and write notes, then when I am *[handwritten: adding to the study value of video lectures is that]*

done, I press play again. You can't do this in class because the *[handwritten: unfortunately, when I space out, during a lecture there's no rewind button]*

teacher will just keep going.

The only thing that is really lacking with video lectures is the ability to interact with the teacher. But you can't do this anyways most of the time because the teacher doesn't like distraction. I used to make WAY to many comments in class. My wife helped me realize that. It was totally compulsive. My hand would shoot up and I would make a comment. Sometimes I would make 25 comments in one class setting. I had a professor come to me once after class and say, "Your comments are very insightful, but we are spending so much time listening to your comments that we aren't being able to finish the lecture." That was pretty embarrassing.

I have worked very hard to learn self restraint to not make so many comments in class, and I am much better than I used to be. I almost have to sit on my hands. Interestingly enough, both of my parents are exactly the same way with making comments in class. Anyway, my point is, when it comes to lectures, the whole "interacting with the teacher" thing is TOTALLY not worth it and doesn't work well for ADHD minds.

Sometimes lectures just can't be recorded. That is okay. You can make your own lecture. All you have to do is get a white board, and write out the material that you are trying to learn into a lesson format. Put some talking points on the white board. Then record yourself giving a 5-20 minute presentation. Then watch yourself giving the presentation. It is the equivalent of reviewing your notes except better. When you watch a recording of yourself, it is more likely to stick because you also recall saying the things which taps into the posterior cingulate gyrus and its autobiographical capacity. Yet, another way to approach this, is to have you and a friend study different pages. Both you and your friend prepare lectures on the material that you need to learn. Have them give their presentation, and record it. Then you can watch it again and again. The repeated

exposures to the material is very helpful.

Part Nine: Using Music While You Study

The posterior cingulate gyrus partially is involved with the
music after stimulates
connection between emotion and memory. Music is able to instill
emotion. If I play music without lyrics, I can study
emotion in us. I have found that if my music has any lyrics,
longer and pay closer attention than when I study without
whatsoever, that the music is a major hindrance to my focus because
music. Lyrics in the music become a major hindrance.
I will be focusing on the words. But if I play music without lyrics, I
drawing my focus away from the subject matter to the
They draw attention
can actually study longer and pay better attention than without
words, when I am reading or doing practice questions
music. I obviously don't listen to music when I am listening to or
I often listen to music. Pandora's "Electronics for Studying"
recording a lecture, but when I am reading or doing practice
Category works well for me. I don't get disengaged (bored)
TEND NOT TO emotionally
questions, I will pull up some music. I have found that going to
The music helps keep my mind engaged enough not to be
Pandora and using their station called "Electronic for Studying"
distracted but not sidetracked enough to prevent
works pretty well for me to make sure I don't get emotionally
me from learning
disengaged (bored). I think the music may also help keep my mind

engaged enough not to be distracted, but not occupied enough to

prevent me from learning things. Whatever the reasons, it works.

Part Ten: Listen Instead of Read

I have shared instances where I found it near impossible to read something. There is a way around this. Sometimes I can't read, but I can still listen. There are a few options here. Many books have an audiobook that goes with it or that you can purchase separately. If you can't do that, you can copy and paste the text of several pages into ttsreader.com (free text to speech) or similar software that will read it for you. You may have to try and find a downloadable version of the book. Lastly if that is not available, try reading the content aloud to yourself, or record yourself reading it.

Conclusion:

Congratulations, you finished the book. There is an appendix at the end that summarizes a few things and adds in some other ideas about brain function. You can read it if you are interested.

I really hope that this book was helpful to you. I have plans to write other books that are specifically designed for educators. An audio recording of this book will soon be available. I have plans to put together online courses that are designed for people with ADHD, as well as educators and parents. The course will include video lectures that teach the ADHD Learning Model and explain the idea of "The Inventive Mind."

Lastly, my hope is to get together with educators and come up with grade school curriculum that is presented in such a way that it follows the ADHD model. Hopefully parents of kids with ADHD can help their kids learn in a way that will be engaging for them and cater to their inventive mind rather than fighting with it.

Appendix

More details about the ADHD brain:

I need to preface this section by saying that this section is really not essential to understand in order to be successful. I included it because I want you to have a good idea of the function of certain brain structures and then correlate them directly to the replicative and inventive mind types. That being said, I do not have a degree in neuroscience and so what I have written is what I understand from my personal studies on the subject.

ADHD, like so many other things, is a diagnosis based on norms. What it is really saying is "We see most people pay attention to things for such-and-such amount of time and they are at a such-and-such level of activity. ADHD people have less attention than that, and more activity than that."

If the percentages of the population were reversed so that 95% of the population had what we now call ADHD, then "normal" people (the other 5%) would be likely diagnosed with "HAHD" (hyper-attentive, hypo-activity disorder). The majority of people would be disturbed at how long the "HAHD" people sat still, how they became so obsessed on one subject that they wouldn't go on to another subject after the normal time of 15 seconds. People might say things like, "Are they partially brain dead or something, they just sit there without climbing all over things like normal kids?"

An ADHD diagnosis is partially just another way of saying that someone is bored of sitting around copying people all day and they want to get up and learn things with their hands through experimentation, trial and error.

I have mentioned the pre-frontal cortex and the posterior cingulate

gyrus previously. I am not in any way pretending to be a

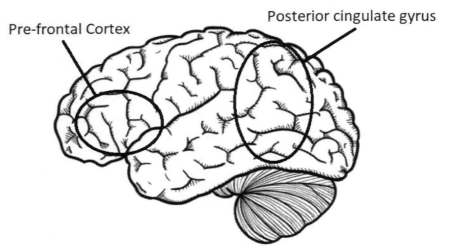

Pre-frontal Cortex

Posterior cingulate gyrus

neuroscientist or specialist in this particular field, but I will do my

best to explain how these areas of the brain operate and then relate it

to the mind of a person with ADHD as I understand it according to

my theory regarding the ADHD mind being an "Inventive mind."

That being said, let's explore these portions of the brain in more

depth.

The posterior-cingulate gyrus is active in the inventive mind (ADHD

mind). It is the part of the brain that connects much of the other functions of the brain together. It is highly related to emotion and memory. Especially spatial memory and autobiographical memory (involving friends and family). The posterior cingulate gyrus is very active during daydreaming. It is theorized to be a dynamic network, and not an unchanging structure. It is thought that the posterior cingulate gyrus is very involved in noticing internal and external differences and facilitating new behavior or thoughts in response. A high level of activity in the posterior cingulate gyrus would result in continued operation with the current cognitive set, while lower activity would be associated with flexibility, exploration and renewed thinking.

I wonder if perhaps this part of the brain transitions in and out of low and high activity in a person with ADHD, perhaps this is what occurs during hyper-focus versus day-dreaming states. I do not know and could not expound extensively on the subject (perhaps this book may motivate such research to occur). The ADHD brain is also highly activated during self-related thoughts. Undistracted, effortless mind-wandering was also associated with posterior cingulate gyrus activation. To me, as I studied the functions of the posterior cingulate gyrus, I could see it related to much of my brain operation.

The pre-frontal cortex is the executive part of the brain. It is the part of the brain that helps us to make decisions based on predictable desired outcomes. It is the part of the brain that gives reason to what most people do. In people without ADHD, the pre-frontal cortex lights up in synchrony with the posterior cingulate gyrus, so that their behaviors are executed in order to attain a predicted desired outcome. When non-ADHD people are undertaking a task, they are able to connect their behavior with the outcome they want. The desired outcome becomes their motivation and it is almost as if they are acquiring their desired consequence, or being rewarded for it as they are doing whatever monotonous activity to attain it. This enables them to do boring and monotonous activities because they are focused on the consequence that they want. When they want a certain outcome, they merely need to replicate the behavior necessary to attain it. For this reason I gave them the name of replicators, because their thought processes are typically manifested through replication. I sometimes state that they have "replicative minds." It is a very good thing to have a replicative mind.

The ADHD brain does not have substantial synchrony between the pre-frontal cortex and the posterior cingulate gyrus. This lack of synchrony has some definite downsides. If you can't synchronize your brain with your pre-frontal cortex, then it becomes very challenging to engage in monotonous activities for the sake of obtaining a predictable desired outcome. You just aren't rewarded for them in the same way that a person with a replicative mind would be. When you are engaged in the activity as a person with ADHD, your brain is not connecting the (often monotonous) behavior with the consequence of the desired behavior and thus drawing motivation to continue engaging the activity because of it. If your brain is not connecting the behavior with the desired outcome very well, then your brain loses intrinsic motivation to continue, it will naturally be drawn to tasks that have some motivation behind them. This has a very interesting side effect. If someone is not drawn to monotonous behaviors due to their predictable outcomes, then their brains will turn towards novelty, discovery, and imagination (daydreaming).

Most humans learn some trade that pays the bills. They continue in their trade for their entire lives because they are cognitively rewarded during their pursuit of the desired consequence. Lacking this cognitive reward for monotony, drives the person with ADHD towards discovery of new things. They seek newness. New ways to do things. New people to talk to. New ideas to dive into. New ways of approaching problems. This is the perfect brain for invention and discovery. I do not know what the ratio of Americans with ADHD is compared to the ratio of non-Americans with ADHD, but if I found out that Americans high a higher ratio of people with ADHD compared to other nations, I might attribute that to genetics. What I mean is that if a new land were discovered, the people who I most visualize being driven to discover it, would be people with ADHD. If I were to imagine a group of people who would oppose the powers of the English government and be defiant against them, regardless of the predicted outcome, I would think that people with higher ADHD tendencies would fit that description. I have wondered if perhaps the many advances that America took during various revolutions was largely due to the higher prevalence of ADHD in America. People who are driven by the pursuit of discovery. Then, much like my father, when they find something of interest to them, their mind becomes hyper-focused and driven towards invention to discover what can be (imagination), rather than what is (predictable outcomes based on the synchrony of the pre-frontal cortex).

People with ADHD minds, or inventive minds tend to challenge the edges. They think outside the box. They come up with exceptions. They resist doing things the same way as everyone else. Not out of spite, but because their mind literally does not function that way. Their brain literally resists reading instruction manuals because it does not connect that monotonous and boring behavior with the desired outcome. Rather their mind drives them towards getting their hands dirty and learning how to do things on their own. This approach is saturated with the possibility of discovery. It is drenched in the higher probability of invention. As I suggested in the story called "The Inventor and The Replicator" perhaps this inventive brain type is perpetuated in the evolutionary gene pool, (or designed), because it promotes the species to have a few minds like that peppered in the general population, to stir the pot of ideas and get humans out of their often stagnant repetitive ways of doing things.

I do not think that anyone's brain is 100% inventive or 100% replicative. I think that there are functional ratios of both within most, if not all people. I think those who struggle to find monotonous tasks rewarding enough to engage in them despite their predicted beneficial consequence, perhaps are more inventive in their brain type. And those who are able to engage in the same repetitive task because they are sure of the predicted reward, may be more replicative. What a wonderful diverse world we live in.

Earlier, I compared replicative minds to dolphins and inventive minds to birds. Most all of the food is in the ocean, where the dolphins live. This symbolizes that most of the rewards are at the end of monotonous activities and monotonous academic pursuits. Dolphins live there in the water, which makes it easy for them to grab the food. Birds must hold their breathe for a quick dive, to get the food. But birds are better at getting that birds-eye view of the ocean. Through their flight, they are better equipped to spot the big schools of fish from the air, even though they are less inclined to go down and get the fish. The birds discover and the dolphins eat. Unless you manipulate the processes of your own brain as a person with ADHD to become a swimming bird, that can discover the fish, and then dive into the water and eat them. The dolphins will eventually find you feasting, and they will replicate and join in, while you go off to find another meal elsewhere (make a new discovery).

Brain Activity in The Replicator:

The type of processing that drives monotonous behavior is from the pre-frontal cortex, where the person repeating the task is doing so out of a motivated reasoning. This is done because they associate this repeated behavior with the attainment of some desired outcome. Therefore, much of the brain activity in a person with a primarily replicative mind will be in their pre-frontal cortex.

Brain Activity in The Inventor:

However, the inventive mind is seeking for discovery and the excitement that comes with it. There is no concrete expected outcome from doing something new because they are seeking experiences outside of their experience through their imagination (daydreaming), they are thus motivated by novelty. Their pre-frontal cortex is not as active because the pre-frontal cortex requires consequence driven behaviors. In other words, they are not doing things which have a previously experienced result. Inventive minds are not driven by the consequence associated thought processes of the replicator, but instead their posterior cingulate gyrus is more active as they get emotional feedback from discovery and are driven by it. It is the emotions associated with discovery that drives them as their posterior cingulate gyrus is active. This does not mean that they cannot learn. It means that the way they learn is different and so the approach to teaching them must be different in order to be effective. The inventive mind wanders from activity to activity. From thought to thought. Much like a bird drifting through the air. It remains like this until it finds something that it can explore. To explore it, the inventive minds must engage with the activity as hands-on as possible. If it finds the activity ripe with possibilities of reward, it may go into project mode: "hyper-focus." This is where the inventive mind is "driven with a motor" to complete the project. It can learn things incredibly rapidly in this state. It can go without food and water and rest for long periods of time without even noticing that it is hungry, thirsty or fatigued. Once the inventive mind completes the task, it goes back to flying again. If the inventive mind is free to fly and free to dive, it can do great things.

The greatest challenge is that in todays society, and in our current education system, often inventive minds are punished for flying and they are punished for diving. When they are flying they are shot down and when they dive they are shot again.

Earlier I specifically stated that I highly doubt that any mind is 100% inventive or 100% replicative. I do contrast these types of minds against each other, but in actuality, everyone has components of both. Some people are just much more inventive than they are replicative and this is why it is challenging for them to learn in learning environments that are tailored for replicative minds only. It probably has to do with how much synchronous communication there is to their pre-frontal cortex. More synchrony means more motivation to be replicative. It definitely doesn't mean that people with total synchrony to their pre-frontal cortex can't be creative or do unique things, or invent things, just as inventive mind is not incapable of replication, it's just not motivated to do this. So replicative minds are capable of doing unique things and discovering new ways to do things but having a replicative mind just means that they may not have as much motivation to do so.

Many people with inventive minds may also have enough of a replicative aspect to their mind (synchrony with their pre-frontal cortex) that they are able to pass school even though it may be painfully boring to them. Some people with nearly pure inventive minds are essentially unable to adjust to replicative learning models. Their drive for novelty and discovery is too overwhelming for them to have success in learning by sitting still and watching other people all day. These kids grow up being told that they are stupid (in the form of grades), because their intelligence is constantly being assessed in terms of their ability to replicate, which is something that their mind is not geared to do well.

If you judged a birds ability to travel solely on its skill at swimming, you might rank it as the worst of all the travelers. Similarly, if you judge the learning capacity of an inventive mind by its ability to learn through replication based learning models, you might rank it as the worst of learners.

Made in the USA
San Bernardino, CA
15 June 2017